Dear S

Much thank... ...
extraordinarily thoughtful ...
and generous gift to New City.
In a word, I was very moved.
I look forward to "next time."
Until then let's be faithful to every
good work God has called us to.

Love,

[signature]
11/01/12

Empowered by Joy

Empowered by Joy

Reflections on Paul's Letter to the Philippians

PAUL S. JEON

WIPF & STOCK · Eugene, Oregon

EMPOWERED BY JOY
Reflections on Paul's Letter to the Philippians

All Scripture quotations are the author's own translation.

Wipf & Stock
An Imprint of Wipf and Stock Publishers
199 W. 8th Ave., Suite 3
Eugene, OR 97401

www.wipfandstock.com

ISBN 13: 978-1-62032-286-4

Manufactured in the U.S.A.

This work is dedicated to Dr. John Kim,
a servant of Christ Jesus
who has empowered countless people
to partner together for the cause of the gospel.

Contents

Foreword by Paul E. Kim • *ix*

Preface • *xiii*

1   Reflections on 1:1a • 1

2   Reflections on 1:1b • 4

3   Reflections on 1:2 • 8

4   Reflections on 1:3–8 • 12

5   Reflections on 1:9–11 • 15

6   Reflections on 1:12–14 • 18

7   Reflections on 1:15–18a • 22

8   Reflections on 1:18b–20 • 25

9   Reflections on 1:21–26 • 28

10   Reflections on 1:27–28 • 31

11   Reflections on 1:29–30 • 34

12   Reflections on 2:1–5 • 38

13   Reflections on 2:6–11 • 42

14   Reflections on 2:12–13 • 46

15   Reflections on 2:14–18 • 50

16   Reflections on 2:19–30 • 54

17   Reflections on 3:1–3 • 57

18   Reflections on 3:4–8 • 61

19   Reflections on 3:9 • 65

20   Reflections on 3:10 • 68

21 Reflections on 3:11 • 71

22 Reflections on 3:12–16 • 74

23 Reflections on 3:17—4:1 • 77

24 Reflections on 4:2–3 • 80

25 Reflections on 4:4–7 • 83

26 Reflections on 4:8–9 • 86

27 Reflections on 4:10–14 • 89

28 Reflections on 4:15–20 • 92

29 Reflections on 4:21–23 • 95

Foreword

THE WORD "devotional" comes from (surprise!) the word "devotion," which, according to the Oxford English Dictionary, means "love, loyalty or enthusiasm for a person or activity." Apropos then that Dr. Jeon's devotional on Philippians is dedicated to Dr. John Kim, whose life embodies a love and loyalty for Jesus Christ as well as a passionate enthusiasm for the activity of exhorting others to have that same love and loyalty. The Global Leadership Development Institute (GLDI), on whose behalf this devotional is written (and where I first met Dr. Jeon), is a testament to this. Dr. Kim's loyalty to Jesus outweighed his dedication to his vocation, which only made him a more distinguished and decorated academian and a trusted adviser to many companies and state and federal officials. "Integrity" is a constant refrain from those that were taught by (and worked with) him. His commitment to our Lord and His beloved bride (the local church) made him a more effective elder in tirelessly serving, building up and unifying the body of Christ (Phil. 1:27c). The church Dr. Kim planted in Alaska—which grew to be the largest Korean-American church in the forty-ninth state—held its first services in his living room and got its start when he would, in the evenings after a long day of work, go door to door asking people to come. Dr. Kim's allegiance to his identity in Christ (and his citizenship in heaven), made him all the more patriotic, willing to stand in the gap for this nation's renewal and revival. And his love of our Savior, surpassing his love for his own family, has only made him a more affectionate and selfless husband, father, and grandfather (I would know since I'm his son). Not a day goes by when we don't talk—and he always ends our conversation with, "I love you." My dad's certified status as a septuagenarian is belied by his infectious energy, the age of his friends and partners in the gospel, his bear hugs, the romance of his marriage to my mom, his teachable-ness, and his constant smile—all because of the joy that comes from his prayerful focus on the Messiah.

Not yet getting off my etymological horse, "devotion" comes from a Latin word meaning "consecrate," or making or declaring something sacred or an object of honor. That is precisely what Dr. Jeon has done in his treatment of Philippians. By taking an originalist view of the text, he has approached the words of Apostle Paul's letter as they ought to be, as God's sacred word. In that regard, Dr. Jeon has written a devotional in God's own words for God's own ends, not his own (not a surprise given who Dr. Jeon is, as I'll mention below). Yes, there is reflection and real-world application worthy of a devotional intended to edify and empower Christian (servant) leaders-in-the-making, but that is done without forsaking a deeper dive into the text. In an age of sound-bites and 140-character limits, it would have been easy, especially in a devotional, to choose feel-good slogans over serious study. Thankfully, Dr. Jeon doesn't succumb—and really, if you truly share in Paul's prayer that your "love may abound more and more, with knowledge and all discernment, so that you may approve what is excellent, and so be pure and blameless for the day of Christ, filled with the fruit of righteousness that comes through Jesus Christ" (Phil. 1:9–11)—would you want it any other way? Refreshingly, there is a delicate reverence in this work without the context-less reinvention. I've been immensely blessed by that reverence, that "holding fast to the word of life." (Phil. 2:16).

I've also been blessed by my friendship with Dr. Jeon. One of the things that I love about him is that he's a man of many accomplishments, but he never takes himself too seriously. And although never having "seen him in action" as one of his congregants, I've always felt that I was under his care. In that way, Dr. Jeon constantly looks to the "interests of others"—whether that's me and my family, his family, his friends and colleagues, his congregants, or to you, the reader, in the pages that follow.

Paul E. Kim
March 17, 2012
Faculty Member, GLDI
Executive Leadership Team
Jesus Awakening Movement for America (JAMA)

Preface

IT IS my privilege to write a brief devotional on Paul's Letter to the Philippians on behalf of The Global Leadership Development Institute (GLDI) and in honor of Dr. John Kim, its founder and president.

First, a word about Dr. Kim. I met Dr. Kim in the summer of 2008 and was immediately struck by his passion for God's glory and his commitment to form partnerships for the sake of the gospel. Dr. Kim is no young buck, but his zeal for the Lord is like that of a new believer. For me, there is no passage that better captures his essence than Philippians 1:18–21: "The only thing that matters, whether from good or bad motive, is that Christ is preached; in this I rejoice. And I will continue to rejoice. . . . It is my expectation and hope that I will not at all be ashamed, but will have full courage so that now, as always, Christ will be exalted in my body, whether by life or by death. For to me, to live is Christ and to die is gain." I, along with many others, thank Dr. Kim for exemplifying a life empowered by joy. I am confident that many generations will benefit from the fruit of his labors.

Now, a word on the devotional. I sought to write a devotional that, on the one hand, is faithful to Saint Paul's original meaning when penning Philippians. There is no shortage of devotionals that compromise the original meaning of the text for the purpose of being inspirational.

I do not intend to be mean-spirited or snooty here. My concern is borne out of the conviction that God's word is most edifying to us when it is rightly understood and then rightly applied. I have encountered many people who have suffered as a result of misunderstanding and misapplying Bible verses and passages. Consider, for instance, how many have taken Philippians 4:13 ("I can do everything through him who strengthens me.") as the basis for pursuing unwise and perhaps even sinful ends, as if Paul were suggesting that we can literally do anything if we just believe. On the other hand, I recognize that the immediate application of what the Bible is saying is not always clear. Therefore, I have attempted to draw out practical and simple applications for those seeking a devotional that speaks into their actual lives.

A word on the proper use of the devotional. All daily devotions should begin with a prayer for illumination and for an increasing commitment to grow in obedience. Christianity, after all, isn't simply about growing in knowledge but growing in obedience. Also, the reader should not only first read the given passage for a particular devotion but should also skim what comes immediately before and after. This will nurture the important habit of reading and interpreting the Bible in context, the most important rule of hermeneutics (the science of Biblical interpretation). Finally, I suggest jotting notes in the book for later reflection. Some thoughts may merit further reflection when time allows.

The selection of the title *Empowered by Joy* is not intended to suggest that this is the only—or even the main—theme of the letter (although it is undoubtedly a prominent theme). Rather, it reflects my belief that many believers are weary and in need of inspiration—and, I daresay, power—to persevere in this race of faith. I thought the example of Paul, one wrongly imprisoned, rejected, and ridiculed by his gospel-colleagues, and confused about what is to happen next, but nevertheless full of joy and unwavering in his commitment to proclaim Christ, whether by life or death, might be of great encouragement to those struggling with fatigue and discouragement. My hope is that your soul would be nurtured, if even in a small way, through this devotional.

As always, some thanks are in order. First, I thank my parents, Chan and Myung, and my siblings, Abraham and Mary. Special thanks to mom. Second, I thank my friends at GLDI for the opportunity to write this devotional. In particular, I am grateful for Cathy Rabb, the most humble wonder worker I have encountered over the years. Third, I thank the members of NewCity church for their patience with the absent-minded professor. You have brought me much pain and pleasure. Finally, I thank my wife and son. I love you both with all I am.

Paul S. Jeon

February 24, 2012

1

Reflections on 1:1a

FELLOW SERVANTS OF CHRIST

P AUL BEGINS his letter to the Philippians by stating the senders as Paul and Timothy. We don't want to overstate the significance of including Timothy, but there are at least two points to notice. First, Timothy, likely Paul's closest missionary companion, shared a special relationship with the Philippians. Luke notes in Acts 18 that Timothy played a special role in the evangelistic efforts in Macedonia, where Philippi is located. For Paul, then, to have omitted Timothy from a letter addressed to the latter's friends would have been surprising. Second, as we'll see, the idea of partnership and unity permeates this letter. It comes as no surprise, therefore, that from the outset Paul would mention Timothy as a way of highlighting that even the great apostle recognizes the necessity and value of partnering with other believers for the work of proclaiming the gospel in word and deed.

In our desire to do great things for the Lord, we often adopt an individualistic approach, illustrating the extent of our culture's influence. Doing great things for God sometimes looks like we're trying to leave a legacy for ourselves. Paul reminds us here that doing great things for God usually requires partnering with other believers. It's instructive that even someone as great as the apostle humbly and frequently acknowledged his need for community. Perhaps we have been turned off by our church experiences or other attempts to work with other believers and Christian organizations, and we suppose that we can accomplish more by going solo. This way of thinking deviates from the example we find in Paul.

The term "servant" has two connotations. On the one hand, it connotes—perhaps to the surprise of some—authority. This isn't simply true for the Old Testament (e.g., Moses, one of the most authoritative figures in Israel's history, is referred to as the "servant of the Lord" [Joshua 1:1]). Even today, Alfred, the famous butler for Bruce Wayne (a.k.a. Batman) has tremendous authority over his household. On the other hand—and I believe this is the connotation the apostle wants to draw attention to here—is that of meekness, humility, and service. It's worth noting that the only other occurrence of the term is found in Philippians 2:7, where Jesus is described as one who emptied himself and took the form of a "servant." In describing himself and Timothy as "servants of Christ Jesus," then, the apostle— who has great authority—is communicating to his audience that servanthood is the best imitation and representation of his master, the ultimate servant-king.

It would be unwise to reduce the imitation of Christ to just one attribute, but none will argue that humility is one of the qualities that should be manifest in every believer. Specifically, just as Christ Jesus revealed himself as a servant who came to seek and save the lost, so too our fundamental identity is that of a servant. In our world, there's tremendous pressure to be at the top of an organization, whether it's at work, church, or even at the home. We want to be "number one." Paul's self-identification as a servant of Christ Jesus, however, is a healthy reminder that if we indeed belong to the great servant-king, then we are to share in that fundamental identity by pursuing a deeper understanding and practice of what it means to be a servant.

Questions for Further Reflection

1. In your efforts to live for Jesus Christ, how much priority do you place on developing gospel partnerships? Name several people you have partnered with over the years and the work you were able to do as a result of such synergy.

2. Consider the awesome truth that Christ Jesus emptied himself of glory to become a servant. As one who belongs to this servant-king, do you represent him well by exhibiting the character and lifestyle of a servant?

2

Reflections on 1:1b

BETWEEN TWO WORLDS

A WOODEN translation of 1:1b would have read something like, "To the holy-ones in Christ Jesus in Philippi." "Holiness" describes a state of being set apart. By virtue of their relationship with Christ Jesus (the theological phrase that's often used here is "union with Christ," but more on that later), believers are set apart from their surrounding world while being immersed in their surrounding world. Hence, the irony and depth of meaning in the first half of 1:b: the Philippians, like all believers, are those who, on the one hand, are "*in* Christ Jesus," and on the other hand, are "*in* Philippi." In short, believers are in the world but not of the world because their identity rests fundamentally in Christ Jesus.

The illustration that's often given to clarify this point goes something like this. Suppose you're a citizen of one country having to reside temporarily in another country for study (perhaps you're an exchange student) or for work (perhaps you're an expat). On a fundamental level, your citizenship and identity rest with your country of origin.

Nevertheless, you're temporarily living in another world. Similarly, believers are those whose fundamental identity is in Jesus and whose citizenship is in heaven. Still, for the time being, they also live in this world (in the case of the Philippians, Philippi).

Two additional observations regarding this short verse: First—perhaps at the expense of reading too much into the text—it's worth noting that Paul adopts the sequence of being "in Christ Jesus" before being "in Philippi." It may have been his subtle way of reminding the recipients of this letter that their primary identity rests not in their immediate and tangible surrounding but in their mystical union with the risen Lord. Second, this dual identity is shared with all the saints. Hence, Paul is careful to include the adjective "all" and to make special note of "the elders and deacons." Just as Paul accentuates the importance of recognizing Timothy as a fellow servant of Christ Jesus, so too the Philippians are to remember that they sojourn in this life with other believers. This perspective stands in clear contrast to some sort of rugged, individualistic view of the Christian faith, as if the only thing that matters is one's personal relationship with Jesus.

Admittedly, it's difficult not to be influenced by our surroundings. Most of us have struggled with this since our youth. If a particular type of clothing or accessory became popular in grade school, then we wanted to make sure that we weren't left behind. Similarly, even when we're grown adults we experience the need to keep up with those around us. If your friends are suddenly buying a condo, you feel that you should be doing the same. If your colleagues at work have adopted a certain lifestyle, you want to do the same in order to fit in. To be sure, we tend to deny that this is the case. But the truth is that while living in the world we can't help but become of the world.

Paul's description of the Philippians isn't intended to suggest that as believers we should isolate ourselves from the rest of the world. Rather, we're to remember, through mutual exhortation and reproof, that we are to march to the beat of a different drummer. Given that our identity is in Christ, we are to live like Christ while being very much immersed in this world. Is this difficult? Absolutely! Most Christians likely suffer from amnesia: the minute they're in the world they forget that they are called to think, feel, speak, and act differently as servants of Christ. This is why regular time reading and reflecting on scripture and pray-ing—and especially fellowshipping with other believers—is so important as we live between two worlds. Through these means of grace we are to remember that first and foremost we are "in Christ" and then "in x-y-z."

Questions for Further Reflection

1. Meditate on the idea of living between two worlds. Make sure you understand what it means to be "in Christ" and "in x-y-z." Try to think of another illustration to deepen your grasp on this important biblical idea.

2. Make a chart similar to the one below, the first column containing various aspects of your life. The second and third columns are labeled "In Christ" and "In x-y-z," where "x-y-z" is the slice of the world in which you are immersed. Then do a survey on the way you think about family, money, sexuality, etc. Check the appropriate box

for each aspect. Finally, determine whether you're living like one whose primary identity is rooted in Christ.

	"In Christ"	"In x-y-z"
Family		
Money		
Sexuality		
Etc.		

3. Returning again to this important theme of partnership, consider whether you place enough emphasis on gospel-community. As we can all attest, we're quick to forget our fundamental identity. It's mainly through the encouragement and rebuke of fellow believers—especially of our elders and deacons—that we remember our calling to shine as lights as we live between two worlds.

3

Reflections on 1:2

POWER AND PEACE

"GRACE" IS often defined as unmerited favor, and this is fine, but it carries different connotations throughout the New Testament. Here in verse two, for instance, it carries the nuance of power. Previously, Paul has already hinted at the notions of grace understood in terms of unmerited favor. Both Paul and Timothy are "servants of Christ Jesus" by grace, i.e., because of God's unmerited favor versus merit. Similarly, the Philippians are saints by virtue of their gracious union with Christ Jesus. In verse two, however, Paul is offering a prayer-wish upon the recipients of this letter, asking for power on their behalf to carry out the exhortations he provides in the letter. Paul, of course, hopes that the letter itself will be a conduit of gracious power. Thus, the Christian life begins and ends with grace. By grace, we have been made holy and now possess our new identity as servants of Christ. And it's grace that empowers us to continue to live in holiness, as we rely on the prayers of other believers and look to Scripture.

"Grace" precedes "peace" because it's' the grace of God that results in peace. We should understand peace on several levels. First and foremost, the unmerited kindness and favor of God results in peace between God and man. Second, the grace of God results in peace between believers. Finally, his grace results in peace between those in Christ Jesus and those outside of Christ Jesus (in this instance, between saints in Christ Jesus and those in Philippi who are outside of Christ Jesus). When thinking of the peace that God offers, it's important for us to appreciate all three nuances. Most importantly, because the peace that Paul has in mind is a peace that comes from God, it will exhibit a unique quality of transcending all understanding (see 4:7). For this reason, we shouldn't be surprised that the peace of God is something that the world simply cannot understand.

We shouldn't be naïve in supposing that the peace of God means we won't ever experience unrest. In fact, as believers we'll often experience hostility as a result of our allegiance to Jesus Christ. Over the years I've met many believers who have been disowned by their friends and family as a result of their faith. Paul isn't suggesting that we'll spontaneously experience a sense of peace with God and actual believers as a result of God's grace. Peace, as Paul indicates in various sections of the letter (e.g., 4:2), requires effort. Nevertheless, it's God's grace that makes any sort of peace possible.

Finally, as we've already noted, grace and peace come from God our Father and the Lord Jesus Christ. It's difficult not to notice the threefold repetition of "Jesus Christ" within these short verses. Paul and Timothy are servants of Christ Jesus. The Philippians are saints in Christ Jesus.

And, now, blessings come from the Lord Jesus Christ. This repetition makes clear that Christ Jesus—specifically union with Christ Jesus ("in Christ Jesus")—not only plays a central role in the life and thinking of the apostle but will also be a key theme in his letter to the Philippians.

Christ Jesus is the anthem of Paul's life. It's literally impossible for him to think of any aspect of life outside of his relationship with Jesus. Anyone who has been in a relationship understands this, and I'm not referring simply to romantic relationships (although this principle is clearly expressed in such relationships). Most parents will say that once you have children, everything revolves around the parent-children relationship. If you're considering vacationing with a newborn, you think of whether your newbie will be able to endure a long flight. If you're considering a night out, you think of who will watch your children. If you're considering a sizable purchase, you wonder how the purchase would impact your child's college fund. In a similar way, once you enter into an authentic relationship with Jesus Christ, the net result should be that it's inconceivable to consider anything outside of your union with him.

Questions for Further Reflection

1. Which do you tend towards: verse 12 or verse 13, an emphasis on human works or an emphasis on divine works? How does this tendency come out?

2. What are two or three thematic sins in your life? How have you been battling them with the kind of initiative and diligence implied in 2:12?

3. As you battle sin in your life, do you do so acknowledging and continuing to rely on "God who works in us to will and work for his pleasure"? Is he the one who continues to empower you, or are you drawing from your limited reserve of determination and ability?

4

Reflections on 1:3–8

GRATITUDE FOR GOSPEL PARTNERSHIP
AND GOD'S FAITHFULNESS

SAINT PAUL had his share of problem churches, churches that were either abandoning his gospel message or engaging in immorality absent even among unbelievers. But the believers in Philippi were a source of tremendous joy for the apostle. Notice how he begins and ends this passage on a positive note: "I thank my God whenever I remember you" (1:3), and, "For God is my witness how I long for all of you with the affections of Christ Jesus" (1:8). The depth of Paul's joy and affection is reflected in the repeated use of the Greek term "all" (seven times!) and its cognates (e.g., "always" in 1:4); it's as if Paul can't fully contain the intensity of his love and gratitude for the Philippians. While other churches gave him ulcers, the Philippians gave him strength to persevere in gospel ministry (1:4).

Paul gives two reasons for his joy. First, he's thankful for their gospel partnership, distinct in its persevering quality and concrete expression: "I thank my God . . . for your gospel partnership *from the first day until now*" (1:5).

In contrast to those who are initially excited by the gospel but then lose their passion, the Philippians have remained by the apostle's side both in his chains and in the defense and confirmation of the gospel (1:7). Paul, therefore, is very thankful for them on a personal level but also—and perhaps even more so—because their persevering quality is evidence of true faith: their personal support for Paul ultimately represents their own commitment to the cause of the gospel. For this reason he says to them, "You are all participants of grace" (1:7).

Second, Paul is full of joy because he's confident in God's faithfulness. Already, the Philippians have exhibited signs of genuine faith, leaving no doubt in Paul's mind that they are true partners for the gospel. Nevertheless, such persevering faith is a sign for Paul that God has, in fact, started a good work in them; and he knows without a doubt that God will bring to completion the good work he has started until the day of Christ Jesus (1:6). In other words, Paul knows that God is a faithful God, never leaving any good work unfinished. Ultimately, then, it's not even the Philippians' track record that elicits so much confidence on Paul's end, but God's faithfulness.

From the beginning of this letter, then, we get a glimpse into Paul's joy. On the one hand, it's not overly spiritual as if Paul is saying that he's joyful simply because of God. Rather, he makes very clear—emphatically so—that his joy stems in large part from the profound fellowship he has with the Philippians. He prays with joy, he reflects with joy, he hopes with joy because they are participants of grace who have supported him in every season of his ministry. In this sense, Paul's joy is immensely "worldly." On the other hand, his joy ultimately comes from knowing that God will undoubtedly finish every good work he has started. Despite whatever current and future struggles there are, one constant is God's constancy, which, in turn, empowers us to be joyful always.

Questions for Further Reflection

1. Notice how Paul remains other-centered even in his suffering. How does Paul's example challenge and inspire you?

2. Reflect on one or two things that are very important to you, perhaps of utmost importance. Would you be able to rejoice if those things were to disappear?

3. What good has God accomplished in your personal sufferings throughout your life?

5

Reflections on 1:9–11

PAUL'S PRAYER TO GROW IN LOVE

I T'S SAFE to say that love today is treated more like a feeling than anything else. Hence, if you fall in love—if you feel intense passion for another person—you get married; if you lose that passion, you separate. Certainly love is a feeling, but it's so much more. Saint Paul reminds us in today's passage that love has a cognitive component: "I pray that your love may abound more and more in *knowledge and discernment*" (1:9). "Knowledge" refers to a general understanding of what love is; "discernment" refers to concrete actions consistent with such knowledge. For instance, we may grow in understanding that love involves forgiveness. Discernment is taking actual and careful steps towards reconciliation.

As we have observed already in the letter, Paul's concern is for the entire community of believers in Philippi. This simple observation makes an important difference in the way we interpret 1:10–11. For example, the statement, "that you may discern what is excellent" (1:10a) isn't referring to making wise personal decisions but pursuing what is most profitable for the entire community. Similarly, the term "blameless" carries the connotation of being inoffensive, that is, seeking a lifestyle that would not offend other believers in the community. Rather than being stumbling blocks to one another, the Philippians are to be "filled with the fruit of righteousness" (1:11a), that is, they are to abound in good deeds towards all the saints, which is evidence of their new righteous status through Jesus Christ.

The ultimate purpose for Paul's prayer and the good deeds that overflow from growing in love is the "glory and praise of God" (1:11b). This final statement echoes what Paul says elsewhere, that "whether you eat or drink—whatever you do, do it all for the glory of God" (1 Corinthians 10:31). Here, Paul is reminding the Philippians that what is really at stake is God's glory. By growing in their ability and commitment to discern what is best for the community and by seeking to remove any possibility for offense, the Philippians demonstrate their commitment to glorify God. The principle is simple but easily and regularly forgotten: loving God and loving the saints are inseparable. The degree to which God is honored in our lives is directly related to the extent of our love for all believers.

Questions for Further Reflection

1. Paul challenges us to think of love not just in terms of a feeling but also in relation to "knowledge and discernment." How does his challenge compare to our culture's approach to love? How does it challenge your own understanding of love?

2. Do you regularly consider how your actions impact other believers in your church? Identify concrete ways you are helping and/or hindering your community of faith. Humbly ask other believers in your church how they believe you are helping and/or hindering the life of your church.

3. God's glory is tied to the quality and quantity of our love for the saints. How does this truth inspire you to persevere and grow in your love for other believers?

6

Reflections on 1:12–14

GOD'S GOODNESS IN THE MIDST
OF SUFFERING

PAUL'S IN prison, and I'm pretty sure that no prisoner is ever happy (even if you get a nice prison cell like the one Martha Stewart stayed in). Yet he remains—borrowing the language of pop psychology—so positive, or, in Christian terms, joyful. Amazing, isn't it! Here we have a man who's trying to do the right thing by remaining a faithful servant of the Christ, and what does he get for it? Prison! Fantastic. Indeed, the Bible is all about health and wealth to those who do the will of God!

Paul's response to his situation ought to leave us speechless. For starters, most of us must admit that when we go through "trial and tribulation," we begin to drown in our sorrow, and the last thing that's usually on our mind is other people. The reality is—and I recognize that this may sound somewhat callous—that suffering often makes us selfish. But notice how Paul begins this section by saying, "Now, I really want *you all* to know . . ." Paul knew that the Philippians were probably anxious about his situation and that some, perhaps, were even beginning to question God's goodness. How could God, after all, allow bad things to happen to good people? What's the deal? Knowing this, Paul immediately draws their attention to the good that God is accomplishing. In a word, even in his suffering, he was other-centered. Now that's pretty amazing, and worth reflecting upon.

Perhaps what's most important to observe is that Paul is able to remain positive because he's already defined what's most important to him. In the second half of 1:12 he writes, "what has happened to me has really served to progress the gospel." What's most important to Paul? The progress, the advancement, the spread of the gospel! And so rain or shine, chains or freedom, Paul can rejoice in his current circumstance because it has become known to everyone that he's in prison for the sake of Christ (1:13) and because most of his gospel-partners have become inspired to speak more boldly on account of his chains (1:14). So, yes, his situation is less than ideal; again, no one likes being in prison. But, no, not even his chains can shackle his joy because the gospel is progressing.

Here we learn an important principle regarding joy: the strength of your joy as a *believer* will depend directly on how important the gospel is to you. If the advance of the gospel is of utmost importance to you, then, like Paul, you'll be able to rejoice even when things don't go the way you hoped or planned because what's most important to you remains intact. If, however, the gospel is important but not most important; if the gospel is secondary to getting into the school of your choice, to getting your dream job, to getting "the one" (that mythical creature), then your joy—if you want to call it that—will always remain an endangered specimen. All of us, therefore, need to take time regularly to reflect on whether anything or anyone has become more ultimate to us than the progress of the gospel.

A final reflection is worthwhile to note from this passage, and we need to be especially careful about how we go about applying the following observation. *Sometimes* in life—not always—God allows us to have some insight into why he allows evil. We should remember that Paul was an apostle and therefore enjoyed some unique insight into God's ways. However, even he wasn't always sure of God's rhyme and reason for allowing this to happen and not that. But in this instance it seems like he's got a good sense of the good that is coming from his suffering—namely that the gospel is spreading among the Roman praetorian guard and that other preachers are becoming more courageous. I imagine that had Paul allowed himself to wallow in his suffering he might not have been able to see the good that God was doing. Again, we want to be careful to avoid trying to completely figure God out. In reality, God's ways are higher than ours; we'll never fully know and understand his purposes. But sometimes it's good to take a step back and consider the good he's doing around us through our suffering.

Questions for Further Reflection

1. Notice how Paul remains other-centered even in his suffering. How does Paul's example challenge and inspire you?

2. Reflect on one or two things that are very important to you, perhaps of utmost importance. Would you be able to rejoice if those things were to disappear?

3. What good has God accomplished through your personal sufferings?

7

Reflections on 1:15–18a

WHAT DOES IT MATTER?

TODAY'S REFLECTION follows on the heels of yesterday's thought concerning how our "predefinition" of joy, i.e., what our source of joy is, relates to our ability to endure any circumstance with happiness and hope. Today's passage concludes on the note of joy: "I rejoice." This is especially surprising given that a certain matter seems to be exasperating Paul's already less than ideal situation of being in prison.

Every now and then you come across someone who always appears rather chipper; and, without being unduly gracious, such a person tends to have a rather naïve outlook on the world. Saint Paul, however, wasn't such a person. He recognized, as our passage indicates, that some people preach Christ with bad intentions and some with good intentions (1:15). In other words, the apostle recognized that for every good preacher out there, there's another who's preaching for prestige, financial gain, power, and so forth. In his situation, there were those that recognized he was appointed for the defense of the gospel and were inspired by his imprisonment to preach the gospel more boldly than ever before (1:16). Then there were those who sought to one-up the apostle by preaching in a way that would exasperate his situation. Perhaps some made snide passing remarks, questioning how the apostle—if, in fact, he were driven by pure motive—ended up in prison. Biblical scholars aren't exactly sure how this particular group was stirring up trouble for the apostle, but the point is that they were making his situation worse.

Taking a step back, all of us who have served within the church in some capacity know the difference between external and internal persecution. It's one thing when someone from the outside ridicules your hard work to build up your local church and community. It's another thing when someone from the inside—a fellow church member, perhaps even your own pastor or elder or deacon—derides your efforts and even questions your motives. I would guess that most of us would be more offended and discouraged by the latter than the former. Similarly, it was one thing for Paul's enemies to imprison him, another thing for those who also preach Christ, as Paul accents in both 1:15 and 17, to seek his suffering. One can easily imagine the discouragement and even bitterness he should have experienced.

However, Paul concludes this section in an astonishing manner: "What does it matter—only that in every way, whether from false or true motive, Christ is proclaimed—and in this I rejoice" (1:18). Paul's attitude is a perfect illustration of the principle of not taking yourself too seriously but instead taking God—his glory, his reputation, his fame—seriously. I imagine if some of us were in Paul's situation we would have said, "Who do these people think they are? Don't they know I'm *the* apostle—the apostle of Christ

Jesus who has been uniquely commissioned to proclaim the gospel to the Gentiles? And that I'm in prison as a result of being faithful to my calling? I'm going to pray one of those imprecatory psalms on their behalf!" But Paul calmly, in an almost matter-of-fact manner, says, "Hey—who cares what they say about me? The only thing that matters is that Christ is being proclaimed and, as result, the gospel is progressing. And because of this I rejoice."

At the end of the day the only thing that really mattered to Paul was the progress of the gospel; hence, his ability to rejoice even in chains, even during persecution from those who should have been his friends. Are you also able to echo with the apostle, "What does it matter—only that Christ is proclaimed!"?

Questions for Further Reflection

1. Come up with your own version of 1:18. Paul says, "What does it matter—only that *Christ is proclaimed*!" What would you say? "What does it matter—only that I get this job, get into this program, get married by this age?" This is really a challenge to "know thyself" so that, in turn, you might experience true transformation via specific repentance.

2. Paul reminds us that rejoicing always does *not* require turning a blind eye to our circumstances. How does this encourage you in your current struggles?

3. Consider the principle of not taking yourself too seriously but taking God seriously. What kind of impact would this have on your life?

8

Reflections on 1:18b–20

FOR MY SALVATION

VERSE 18 ends on mixed note: "Indeed, I will rejoice." It's almost as if Saint Paul takes a break to reflect on the fact that his situation is unlikely to change in the near future (although many translations of 1:19a suggest that Paul will soon be "delivered" out of prison). What does a person do when he/she knows with a fair degree of confidence that the bad situation isn't about to change and may, in fact, get worse? Paul's response is, "I will rejoice." Why is this the case? How is it that Paul is able to rejoice even now?

First, Paul can rejoice because he knows—he's absolutely sure—that his current situation is for his salvation, i.e., for his sanctification (1:19). (Note: the term "salvation" has three senses in the New Testament. In terms of the past of being fully forgiven through Christ, "salvation" is described as "justification"; in terms of the present of being made more like Christ, "salvation" is described as "sanctification"; in terms of the future of being made perfect like Christ, "salvation" is described as "glorification.") In short, through this extremely difficult circumstance of being imprisoned and of being persecuted by other preachers, God is refining Paul. Paul is confident that God hasn't left him to rot in prison but even now is doing a good work.

Second, Paul is able to persevere through the prayers of other believers and the help of the Spirit of Christ (1:19b). We often think of people like Paul as supermen who are so thick-skinned that nothing in life impacts their faith. Rain or shine such people rejoice in the Lord. Paul, however, was not that naïve. Very plainly he says, "I'm able to persevere because of your prayers on my behalf and because of the strength given by the Spirit of God." In other words, he highlights that the source of his strength to persevere with joy comes outside of himself. "*You* strengthen me through your prayers. *God* strengthens me through his Spirit." It's a sobering thought that our prayers actually matter and that perseverance itself is a divine work.

Finally, Paul perseveres in his sanctification because he has already decided what he hopes will happen when he stands before God (the language of "expectation and hope" belong to the day when Christ returns). He hopes that God will say, "Paul was never ashamed of the gospel, but with full courage continued to extend Christ in his body, both in life and in death" (1:20). Indeed, the power of the future on how we live in the present is uncanny! Athletes will put their body through hell—and will rejoice in the process— as they envision becoming champions. Parents will work themselves almost to the point of death—and will rejoice in the process—as they envision a better life for their children. Students will stay up endless hours studying—and will rejoice in the process (sometimes)—as they envision the day of becoming a successful professional. How much more, then, can all believers persevere with joy in the present as they long for the day when God will say that we did not lose heart; we were not ashamed of the gospel, but continued in our labors so that Christ would be extended to the nations! May your eager expectation and hope echo that of the apostle!

Questions for Further Reflection

1. God is committed to our sanctification—to our becoming more like Christ—and often uses adversity to accomplish this. How does this beautiful truth help you to rejoice always?

2. Paul, the "super-apostle," isn't shy about expressing his continual need for prayer and the Spirit's empowerment. How are you engaged in regularly asking other believers to pray for you and pursuing divine empowerment?

3. Is it your eager expectation and hope that Christ will be exalted in your life and death? If so, what impact should this have on your current struggles? If not, what impact does that have on your current struggles?

9

Reflections on 1:21–26

FOR ALL THE SAINTS

ONE OF my lifelong commitments is to remain a student of Saint Paul. His letters continue to inspire and humble me. Over the past years, I've become especially challenged by the apostle's love for and devotion to all the saints. Today's passage illustrates what I mean.

Many are familiar with verse 21 ("For me, to live is Christ and to die is gain.") as it's been incorporated into a number of worship songs. What's perhaps less known is how the verse works in the context of 1:21–26. On the one hand, Paul makes it unambiguously clear that—speaking on a personal level—he wants to die so that he can depart from this world of disease, death, and decay, and be with Christ, the lover of his soul (1:23b). It's easy to empathize with Paul. After all, how many of us would prefer the slums of an inner city compared to an all-inclusive beach resort? The choice is obvious.

What's striking, therefore, about the passage is Paul's statement in 1:22–23a. After laying down the options of life and death (1:21), he concludes 1:22 with the expression,

"Yet, what shall I choose I cannot tell," and then goes on to say in 1:23a, "I am hard pressed between the two." Come again—didn't we just note that the choice is obvious? Didn't the apostle himself just admit that "to be with Christ is better by far" (1:23b)? Why, then, is Paul "hard pressed"?

Here we gain tremendous insight into the apostle's heart, specifically his love for the saints. Paul, ever self-aware, knows that his ministry is impactful, i.e., his presence matters for the faith of many. This is why he unabashedly says in 1:25–26 that the faith and joy of the Philippian believers will abound as a result of his coming to them again (see also his statement concerning "fruitful labor" in 1:22). And so—without being unduly confident—he says in a somewhat matter-of-fact way, "To remain in this body—to live—is more necessary for you" (1:24). In summary, knowing that the Philippian believers would benefit from his return and ministry is why Paul is indecisive and hard-pressed. Obviously, he wants to depart and be with Christ in perfect bliss, but his love and concern for the Philippians is so powerful that he feels trapped in what should otherwise be an easy choice.

On a superficial glance, it almost appears that Paul loves the saints more than Christ. Obviously this isn't the case—that would be idolatry. But his love and concern for them is so profound that one could make the confusion. And this should come as a tremendous challenge to us today who often think that it's perfectly acceptable to love Christ but to disregard the Church, which is his body; to suppose that all is well as long as my individual walk with the Lord is strong. Paul, however, entertained no such false dichotomy. In fact, he understood that God is glorified when we live to edify the saints who, in turn, boast all the more in Christ because of our ministry to them (1:26).

Questions for Further Reflection

1. If you could have just one thing, what would it be? Think carefully about this and avoid the Christian-cliché answer. (It's a good practice to regularly ask yourself this question as the answer will provide a good window into what rules your heart.)

2. Do you love your local church? Can other local church members attest to your sacrificial living for the sake of their edification?

3. Consider the relationship between God being glorified and your serving the saints. Reflect on how you are currently causing others to boast in Christ Jesus on account of your personal ministry to them.

10

Reflections on 1:27–28

WORTHY OF THE GOSPEL

We often think of "doing spiritually well" in terms of the number of quiet times done in a week. This isn't necessarily a bad thing, but it sometimes suggests that as long as we're spending a few minutes with the Lord each day, all is well. It doesn't matter how we live the rest of the day—the important thing is that we're doing our quiet times.

Granted, this description is somewhat of an exaggeration, but it gets at the point that sometimes we miss the basic truth that being a follower of Christ is a full-time affair; that it entails a complete directional change in life: we were once headed "this" way, but now we're headed "that" way. This sort of 180-degree turn gets at the core of the exhortation in 1:27a: "Let the manner of your life be consistent with the gospel of Christ Jesus." That is, live each day and each hour as citizens of heaven; let your daily conduct be worthy of the gospel. That Saint Paul advocates such a comprehensive understanding of the Christian life—a "hardcore," all-or-none approach—is highlighted in the statement, "so that whether I come and see you or am absent—irrespective of what happens—I may hear that you are standing firm in one spirit" (1:27b).

In the verses that follow, Paul identifies several aspects of living worthily. First, living as citizens of the gospel requires a tremendous amount of intentionality. It requires going against the current of living for sex, money, and power. Unsurprisingly, Paul uses the phrase "*contending with one soul for the faith of the gospel*" (1:27c) to highlight the struggle involved with living intentionally. Second, living in a manner worthy of the gospel includes striving for unity among the saints. Verse 27 ends by repeating this theme: "standing in *one* spirit, contending with *one* soul for the faith." Honoring Christ includes making every effort to keep and strengthen the unity of the saints. Finally, living as citizens of heaven means persevering in the face of persecution (1:28a). Such a conflict should remind believers of the epic struggle between God and Satan—but also provide opportunity for remembering that God has already triumphed in Jesus Christ and will someday renew all of creation, as Paul's gospel declares. Our perseverance, then, is an expression of our faith that those who trust God will ultimately enjoy salvation, while those who oppose him will experience destruction.

We were taught at a young age that you don't jump over a bridge just because everyone else is doing so. Perhaps what we didn't learn as well is that we're not free, therefore, to live however we please. Rather, as Christians, we belong to Christ: we are citizens of heaven and therefore are called to adopt a life that is worthy of the gospel. This means that we're always asking the question of whether my decision here and now, big or small, fits with the identity of being a citizen of heaven. This means that we're always striving to promote the unity of the church (this takes a lot of work). This means that we're persevering in the face of opposition because we know how the chips will ultimately fall. And we do all this always holding firmly to the conviction that God is in full control of all things (1:28b).

Questions for Further Reflection

1. The Christian life is an all-or-none affair. Do you adopt different identities in different settings and social networks? Or do you live consistently as a citizen of heaven in every situation and in every season of life?

2. Consider the several applications of being a citizen of heaven—living intentionally, pursuing unity, and persevering in opposition. What would these look like in your life right now?

3. What areas in your life do you still treat as yours, i.e., outside of Christ's rule? What daily practices are inconsistent with being a citizen of heaven?

11

Reflections on 1:29–30

GOSPEL-SUFFERING

GETTING A handle on suffering is one of the more difficult—but also one of the more important—Christian
disciplines. But before we consider Saint Paul's perspective
on suffering, let's clarify the kind of suffering he has in
mind. There's suffering in this world that's simply hard, if
not impossible, to explain: an unborn child and mother die
in a car crash after a church meeting; cancer strikes the only
daughter of parents that struggled with infertility for many
years; a tsunami hits a village and wipes away hundreds of
lives in a matter of seconds. There's also the kind of suffering
that comes from our own sinfulness: we made an unwise
decision about having sex outside of marriage and, in the
process, contracted an incurable disease; we gambled away
our lifesavings after drinking too much; we made promises
that we were unable to keep.

These are just some examples of the various faces of
suffering. The suffering that Paul has in mind is the kind that
comes from following Jesus, what I've sometimes dubbed
as "gospel-suffering." As 1:28 from yesterday's meditation

indicates, the believers in Philippi were undergoing persecution and, as a result, were tempted to become frightened.
Paul encourages them not to be afraid, reminding them
that God is in full control (1:28b). In today's passage he
goes on to remind them that they should view suffering as a
blessing from God, as suffering is part and parcel of being a
disciple of Jesus Christ.

Several important comments are in order for 1:29.
First, when suffering for the gospel, we need to remember—as we've already noted—that God is in full control.
The passive form of the verb in verse 29 ("it has been graciously given to you") highlights that God is the ultimate
giver of both faith in Christ and suffering for Christ. In
other words, our suffering for the gospel doesn't come as a
surprise to God as if he were suddenly blindsided. Knowing
that even in suffering God is in control makes a tremendous
difference on how we deal with it. Second, the verb suggests
that suffering is just as much an expression of God's favor as
is the gift of faith. As people who believe that God is good
and in full control, we can say—not just as a cliché, but with
full confidence—that good will come out of our suffering
for the gospel. Third, in our suffering for the gospel we must
always remember that we are suffering for Christ, the one
who suffered for us to a degree that we will never know.
Remember that our suffering in ministry is for the sake
of the one who suffered and died for our salvation puts all
gospel-suffering in perspective.

What I've found especially helpful for getting a handle
on these principles of gospel-suffering is remembering that
gospel-suffering is a norm for believers. This is basically
Paul's exhortation to the Philippians: "Note that you're hav-

ing the same struggle that you saw in me and hear that I still have" (1:30). Jesus himself made it very clear that anyone who wants to follow him must be willing to talk up his cross and walk the road of Calvary. Jesus never suggested that following him would result in your best life now. In fact, his message was that "no servant is greater than his master." Thus, if the master was persecuted and suffered, should the servants be surprised if they share in a similar fate? Similarly, Paul reminds his partners for the gospel that it shouldn't surprise them at all that they're undergoing the sufferings the apostle has experienced.

Questions for Further Reflection

1. How would you categorize your suffering? Are you suffering for the sake of the gospel or are you suffering simply because of your own sin? Perhaps you're suffering in ways that will simply require faith that God's ways are higher than ours. Take time to reflect on the kind of suffering you've endured, or are enduring.

2. "I believe—help me in my unbelief." This is one of my favorite prayers, especially during times of suffering when I believe that God is in full control but need help in my unbelief. Has your suffering tempted you to entertain the belief that God is smaller than your problems and sorrow or that God is no longer accomplishing good? Meditate on this prayer and ask God to empower you with joy.

3. Meditate on Christ's sufferings on your behalf. How does that put your suffering in perspective? Similarly,

meditate on the sufferings of other believers who have struggled for the sake of the gospel. How does that put your suffering in perspective?

12

Reflections on 2:1–5

UNITY THROUGH
CHRIST-EMPOWERED HUMILITY

Just a few verses earlier (1:27) Saint Paul alluded to his concern for working towards Christian unity ("standing firm in *one spirit*, striving together with *one mind*"). In today's passage, he returns to this theme, pleading with the believers in Philippi to fight for peace, especially during this trying time. The command, "Complete my joy" (2:2a) suggests that despite all that the Philippians have done for Paul, thus bringing him much encouragement, the apostle's joy is somewhat tenuous because of the seeds of disunity he detects among them. Surely, there would've been little reason for him to exhort them "to be of the same mind, to have the same love, to be united in soul and thinking" (2:2b) unless there were issues of disunity already brewing. The earnestness with which he pleads comes out in 2:1 where he prepares the way for the command in 2:2a by asking, "If, indeed, there is any encouragement in Christ, any comfort from love, any fellowship with the Spirit, any affection and compassion . . ." (2:1). Paul's like a mother on her death bed pleading to her child, "If you love me and want to honor my life—if, indeed, you want to please me, then . . ."

The key to Christian unity is humility, as expressed rhythmically in 2:3–4: "Do nothing out of rivalry and vainglory, rather in humility consider one another as more significant than yourselves; look not only your own interests, but also to the interest of others." What may have tinged a nerve with the Philippian believers is Paul's suggestion that they're conducting themselves like the false preachers who proclaim the gospel out of envy and rivalry (1:15–17). This innuendo must have been difficult for the Philippians to receive, given the care they extended to Paul (how much more difficult must it have been for Paul to give!). Paul's subtle remark here is a sobering reminder that even the best of us are not insusceptible to the sin of selfishness—of counting ourselves, our wants, our needs, and our interests as more significant than the wants, needs, and interests of others. To be sure, we'll try to explain away our behavior as being a matter of legitimate difference; and while sometimes this may be the case, more often than not disunity is a result of immaturity and selfishness.

The power to be humble rests in Christ. A helpful paraphrase of 2:5 reads something like, "Have this mindset among you, which is fitting for those who are in Christ Jesus." Anyone who tries to be humble by focusing on being humble has already lost, because the moment he thinks he's humble, he's become boastful of his accomplishment. No, humility doesn't come through our own effort and moral fiber. Rather, humility is possible only by becoming a new creation by joining oneself to Christ through faith. What Paul's saying here isn't even, "Be humble," but, "Apply the new mindset that is now yours through Jesus Christ." Again, a person never becomes humble through his own effort. Rather, humility comes to those who have knelt before the cross of Jesus Christ and have asked him to enable them to be and do what they could otherwise not be and do on their accord. Philosophically, Paul's exhortation here could be expressed in terms of, "Be in community (be humble) what you already are in Christ Jesus (one with a new mindset)."

Christian unity, which is an expression of the reconciling power of the gospel, requires humility, which is the antithesis of selfishness. But all of us suffer from the selfish gene. By nature, whether we're infants fighting for toys or adults fighting in marriage, the anthem of our lives is, "It's all about me." The irony is that the more you mature as a believer, the more aware you become of your selfishness. We're just wired to count our wants, needs, and interests as more important than those of others. Being honest and sober about this reality is an important first step towards humility. Similarly, we need to be honest and sober about the fact that selfish people can't suddenly deprogram themselves to be selfless people. This is like asking a scorpion not to sting. We are what we are, and left to ourselves we would be without hope. But thanks be to God that in his Son we have been made anew such that we're now able to look to the cross for both inspiration and power to love, care for, and forgive one another with the mindset of Christ.

Questions for Further Reflection

1. Christian unity is a struggle dealt with by almost every church in every generation in every place. Reflect

on some of your own experiences with disunity in the church. Was humility absent or present among the differing parties? Have you been humble in the way you have handled your differences at church?

2. Describe an instance when you saw humility practiced, a situation where someone actually counted the wants, needs, and interests of others as more important. What impact did it have on the other person? What impression did it leave you with?

3. The irony of the cross is that it "bids me come and die and find that I may truly live."[1] Consider how this irony is especially true with respect to humility. Think about how we grow in humility not by looking within but without, not by looking internally but externally.

1   Tomlin, Chris, and Isaac Watts, et al. "The Wonderful Cross." Lyrics. worshiptogether.com songs, 2000.

13

Reflections on 2:6–11

HUMILITY AND EXALTATION

Today's passage falls within the category of scriptures that you really must memorize and continue to meditate on throughout your life. As we noted yesterday, growing in humility entails growing in Christ. In today's passage we are given one of the best windows into the mindset of our Lord and Savior. Again, I strongly encourage making this one of your "life passages," i.e., a passage that deeply influences your mindset and approach to life.

The first half of the passage (2:6–9) reflects on Christ's humility as expressed in his humiliation. Verse 6–7a reflects with awe on the fact that Christ Jesus, even though in very nature God and thus King of kings and Lord of lords, did not regard equality with God a thing to be grasped, but emptied himself of glory by taking the form of a servant in the incarnation (the taking on human likeness). This is astounding! A weak analogy is found in the CEO who gives up all his prestige, power, and wealth to become the new intern who fetches coffee and makes copies despite his Ivy League degree. Unheard of—indeed! And as if this were not enough Jesus took it a step further by becoming obedient to the will of God even to the point of death (2:8a)! And as if this were not enough he humbly accepted a criminal's death—death on the cross (2:8b)! All this, again, even when he was in nature God! In the words of that old song, "I am speechless, I'm astonished and amazed / I am silenced by your wondrous grace."[1]

Saint Paul's life was all about honoring Christ, and one of the ways he sought to do this was through imitation (imitation, after all, is the greatest form of flattery). As we've already seen and will see more of later in this letter, Paul himself was no ordinary Joe (highly educated and exceptionally gifted). Yet, by adopting the mind of Christ, he cast away anything that was formerly precious to him and adopted the identity of a servant and became obedient even to the point of death, as we see in this letter. In other words, Christ provides a lens for understanding the life of Paul much in the same way Paul's life exemplifies Christ's own humility.

Christ's story, however, doesn't end with his death (thankfully!). The second half of today's passage (2:9–11) reflects on God's faithfulness to Christ's faithfulness: "For this reason, God highly exalted him and bestowed on him the name that is above every name" (2:9). To highlight the comprehensive quality of Christ's reign, Paul adds that "at the name of Jesus *every* knee should bow, *in heaven, on earth, and under the earth*, and *every* tongue confess that Jesus Christ is Lord" (2:10–11). By emptying himself of glory and submitting himself to death, Christ was trusting fully in the Father's faithfulness. God, in turn, remembered

1 Chapman, Steven Curtis. "Speechless." Lyrics. Sparrow, 1999.

the Son's obedience and honored it accordingly. In this way, God's faithfulness to Christ's faithfulness results in "the glory of God the Father" (2:11b).

Having the mindset of Christ involves not only humility, but also full confidence in the Father's faithfulness, which results in the Father's glory. Of course we should seek to grow in humility by considering not only our own interests but also the interests of others; Paul himself exemplifies this. But Paul also exemplifies the faith and confidence of the Son in the Father, a faith and confidence expressed in the apostle's willingness to die for the gospel. Just as Christ trusted that God would vindicate him, so too Paul trusted that God would someday honor his own sufferings. And just as Paul trusted God, so too are we, who have the mindset of Christ Jesus, to believe that all the work we do for the progress of the gospel is never in vain. In full faith—even to the point of death—we labor, confident that someday God will also exalt us and, in this way, bring glory to himself.

Questions for Further Reflection

1. Commit to memorizing Philippians 2:5–11 (I've included verse 5 as it highlights the application of verses 6–11).

2. Meditate on Christ's humility as expressed in his humiliation (2:6–8). Think of one or two analogies that illustrate the wonder of Christ's incarnation. How does your life exemplify Christ's humility?

3. Meditate on Christ's humble confidence in God's faithfulness and, in turn, God's faithfulness to honoring the Son's obedience (2:9–11). How does your life exemplify

Christ's humble confidence? What would "obedience even to the point of death" look like for you?

14

Reflections on 2:12–13

WORKING OUT SALVATION: WHOSE WORK?

OUR PASSAGE today has sparked a considerable amount of scholarly debate. Is Saint Paul suggesting here that we're ultimately responsible for our salvation? What does it mean to "work out our salvation with fear and trembling" (2:12)? Or is Paul using hyperbolic language while knowing that salvation is completely the work of God (2:13)? Before reflecting on these two verses, it'll be helpful for us—to avoid needless confusion—to establish some givens. First, for Paul nothing is more fundamental than the conviction that a person is *not* saved from works but by faith alone. As much as many would like to believe that we in some shape or form contribute to our saving righteousness, this simply is not the case according to Paul. Second, the term "salvation," as we've noted already elsewhere, need not be limited to justification—the establishment of a right relationship with God. It also includes present (sanctification) and future (glorification) aspects; hence, theologians often explain "salvation" in terms of God's *comprehensive* work of redemption. Within this broader sense, our effort to manifest righteousness, especially in the context of our Christian community (2:1–5), is especially important to bear in mind. Third, despite attempts to highlight verse 12 over verse 13 or vice versa, pitting human activity against divine sovereignty, the point here is that both are equally stressed without any reservation from the apostle. Therefore, instead of seeking a resolution to satisfy our own preferences and beliefs, it's best to accept and appreciate the juxtaposition of divine sovereignty and human activity.

One should not blunt the force of verse 12. There are many believers, after all, who adopt an incredibly passive approach to growing in holiness. They suppose that because God wants them to be holy, he'll accomplish it according to his timing, purpose, and power. While there isn't a concerted effort to sin more, there is also little effort to sin less. Pornography, self-absorption, and rudeness are accepted as "just the way I am." Such reliance on grace brings no honor to God's grace but simply cheapens it. Over against this perspective Paul exhorts believers to "work out their salvation with fear and trembling." In fact, a more literal translation of the main verb at hand is "accomplish, bring about, effect, produce," thus making the reading, "Accomplish your salvation." It's astounding, unnerving, and cause for a moment's pause that Paul, who maintains that salvation is "from grace to grace," would describe salvation as something we bring about. We must take extraordinary care not to dismiss the apostle's exhortation to take a conscious and active stance with respect to our sanctification, especially with respect to nurturing the mindset of Christ (2:5).

Still, having highlighted the importance and necessity of human initiative, Paul also stresses God's activity in making possible all our efforts. In verse 13 he writes, "For it is God who works in you both to will and to work for his pleasure." All human activity, then, is to be understood not in terms of seeking to gain favor with God but in humble recognition that all the good we do is because God has made it possible. That human activity is dependent on divine activity is accented in four ways in verse 13. First, the conjunction "for" has a causal force to it, communicating that our work is made possible by God. Second, there's an obvious play on words with the repetition of "work" in the beginning and end of the verse to make the point that God is the one who works our working. Third, Paul penetrates beyond our visible work to our will, highlighting that even the desire to change and grow must be attributed to God. Finally, the closing phrase "for his pleasure" is a reference to God's sovereignty, reiterating the role of divine grace upon all that we will and do. Hence, we can rightly declare that "from him and to him are all good things."

We always run the danger of running down one of two trails. There is, on the one hand, the tendency to overemphasize human effort so that we begin to think along the lines, "God helps those who help themselves," or, "At the end of the day our salvation is really up to us." This approach of highlighting merit has created enough trouble for the church and shows no signs of disappearing for good. On the other hand, we may highlight the primacy of God's grace so that we lose the force of what Paul is saying in 2:12 to achieve our own salvation. We suppose, "God, after all, is in full control, so what does it matter what I do or don't do? Let God be God." Hence, we allow sin to persist without any real battle. God is pleased with neither. Today's passage is a much needed reminder that both human and divine activity are to be held together without highlighting one at the expense of the other.

Questions for Further Reflection

1. Which do you tend towards: verse 12 or verse 13, an emphasis on human works or an emphasis on divine works? How does this tendency come out?

2. What are two or three thematic sins in your life? How have you been battling them with the kind of initiative and diligence implied in 2:12?

3. As you battle sin in your life, do you do so acknowledging and continuing to rely on "God who works in us to will and work for his pleasure"? Is he the one who continues to empower you, or are you drawing from your limited reserve of determination and ability?

15

Reflections on 2:14–18

BE WHAT YOU ARE

YESTERDAY'S REFLECTION focused on the mystery of, on the one hand, working to achieve our salvation, and on the other hand, recognizing God's sovereignty in all that we desire and do. The center of verse 15 reflects both these aspects under the phrase "children of God without blemish." On the one hand, the very fact that we are children of God highlights that God has already achieved salvation by adopting us into his family. On the other hand, the state of being "without blemish"—more specifically, "blameless and pure" in comparison to the surrounding "crooked and perverse generation"—comes about through our effort, specifically the work of striving to "do everything without grumbling and disputing" (2:14). In this regard, the basic exhortation that Saint Paul gives to all believers is, "Be what you already are," i.e., given you're already children of God, conduct yourself in a manner that is fitting and reflective of this divine identity. Our strivings for holiness, then, are not in order to *become* holy but because we already *are* holy. Paul's exhortation is similar to the gentle and encouraging words of a father who has recently adopted a child: "You're no longer an orphan, and so make every effort to live as my son—not in order to become my son but because you already are my son."

The sins of "grumbling or disputing" should bring to mind the days of Israel's wandering in the wilderness (see Exodus 15:24) when the Israelites murmured against God by challenging Moses. Recall how Paul began this letter by noting the leaders among the Philippians: "Paul and Timothy, slaves of Christ Jesus, to all the saints in Christ Jesus in Philippi *with the elders and deacons*" (1:1). This specific reference to the church leaders may have been Paul's way of affirming their authority given a situation where their authority may have been challenged, as 2:14 suggests. In short, it may be that just as the Israelites had complained against Moses, so too the Philippians were beginning to grumble against their leaders. The encouragement to "do everything without grumbling and disputing" is likely referring to the kind of grumbling and questioning that is epidemic of churches today. This, of course, is not to suggest that church members shouldn't provide feedback and input to their leaders and, at times, even challenge them when they are acting sinfully; but, on the whole, leaders who are "holding fast to the word of life" (2:16) should be respected and followed. By serving in every sense without complaining and quarreling, believers "shine as stars in the universe" (2:15).

It is worthwhile to consider how Paul seems to re-turn repeatedly to this theme that one of the ways we most honor God is by our commitment and ability to live in community, whether it's considering the interest of other saints above our own or submitting to those who have been placed over us as elders and deacons. Simply put, how we love and respect one another will very much impact our effectiveness as lights in the world. If we simply do as the world does by pursuing first and foremost our own needs and by holding those in authority with contempt, then believers are no different from the darkness surrounding them. If, however, we respect one another and revere our spiritual leaders in obedience to Christ, we show that we are truly unique as children of God. This thought should be especially sobering for those who perhaps overemphasize how they, as individuals, will honor God while holding their community commitments and conduct in low regard.

Paul concludes this passage with a personal appeal and encouragement. First, in verse 16 Paul expresses his hope that he will "boast on the day of Christ that I did not run in vain and labor in vain." It's as if Paul is communicating to the Philippians, "For my sake be faithful—that I may boast as a result of your perseverance on the day of Christ that my labors were not in vain." This reminds us how much Paul was personally invested in his ministry. Second, Paul acknowledges the "sacrificial offering" (probably referring to a monetary gift) that was given by the Philippians according to their faith and basically says, "It's okay if I ultimately die while doing the ministry which you have made possible through your financial contributions and emotional and prayerful support. I'm thankful for this and rejoice with you all, even as you should be thankful and rejoice with me" (2:17–18). Mutual rejoicing in the face of persecution and even death is possible when believers remember and remind one another of the day of Christ when all will say that nothing done in faith for the progress of the gospel was in vain. May this hope empower you with joy to serve with diligence and perseverance!

Questions for Further Reflection

1. How does your identity as one who is already a child of God change the way you approach God, the world, and others? Do you find that you live out of that identity as a child of God, or do you live as an orphan?

2. Do you respect those in authority, especially the elders, deacons, and pastors of the church? Take time to reflect on whether you are providing constructive feedback or adopting a spirit of criticism. Does your church tend toward grumbling or disputing, like Israel grumbled against Moses?

3. How have church splits and controversies impacted the church's overall ability to shine as lights in the universe and to share the gospel? How might our commitment to love one another and bear with one another's weaknesses open channels for dialogue with unbelievers?

16

Reflections on 2:19–30

MODELS OF GODLINESS

A LMOST EVERYONE, Christian or not, has heard the general advice, "You need role models in your life." What I've found very alarming is that many Christians have few—if any—godly models in their lives. There are various reasons for this, whether it's because we ourselves are too busy to pursue mentors or to mentor younger believers, or perhaps even because we have a gross overestimation of our own spirituality and thus have concluded that there's no one immediately around us who could serve as a true mentor. Setting aside whatever reasons we have, legitimate or not, we're reminded in today's passage of the importance of having people who not only proclaim the gospel but also model the gospel. Here, we're given the examples of Timothy, Epaphroditus, and Paul.

The first half of this section (2:19–24) contains a brief explanation of why Paul has not yet sent Timothy to check in on the Philippians (2:23). This explanation provides Paul with an opportunity to express his high esteem for his spiritual son: "For I have no one like him" (2:20a). Regarding

Timothy, Paul says two things that are especially noteworthy. First, in contrast to "all who seek their own interest, not
the interests of Christ" (2:21)—a reference perhaps to the
ill-motivated preachers noted in 1:15 and 1:17—Timothy is
"genuinely concerned for the Philippians" (2:20b). Second,
in partnership with Paul, Timothy has "served as a slave for
the gospel" (2:22). In these respects, Timothy models obedience to the exhortations given in 2:1–5 and a life wholly
devoted to the progress of the gospel (1:18).

Similarly, Epaphroditus is extolled in the second half
of the section (2:25–30) as Paul's "brother and fellow-work-
er and fellow-soldier" (2:25). Like Timothy, Epaphroditus
is not unduly concerned with his own interests but with the
interests of others. Paul notes that he was "anxious because
the Philippians had heard that he was ill" (2:26), and that
he had labored to meet the needs of the apostle which the
Philippians themselves were unable to fill (3:30). In addition—and most noteworthy—Epaphroditus became ill
(2:27) and even risked his life for the work of Christ (2:30).
Unsurprisingly, Paul encourages the believers in Philippi to
esteem Epaphroditus and men like him who make it their
goal to honor Christ, whether in life or in death (1:20).

Finally, we have the example of Paul himself. Paul's
twofold purpose in this section is to clarify any possible
misunderstanding for not sending Timothy sooner (2:19,
23) and to alleviate the Philippians of any anxiety they
might have as a result of Epaphroditus's illness (2:28). In
other words, Paul was being mindful of other believers—
things that could potentially stumble them, things that were
causing them frustration and anxiety, things that would
effect joy. This, again, is especially astounding given how

Paul's circumstances might have inclined him to become self-absorbed and to throw a pity party for himself. But even now, in his suffering, his concern is for the wellbeing of the Philippians. Simply amazing how the gospel brings about such power and love!

The challenge for us today is to have such models of true spirituality and to hold them in high esteem. Do you have models like Timothy, Epaphroditus, and Paul who demonstrate what it means to put the needs of others above their own and who risk it all for the work of Christ? Do you have people who labor to advance the joy of the gospels in the lives of others and who themselves are empowered by the joy of the gospel? May the Lord richly surround you with models of godliness!

Questions for Further Reflection

1. Name several models of godliness in your own life. How have they shaped who you are today and the pursuits of your life? Be as specific as possible.

2. If you don't have models of godliness, what steps can you take to change this state? (It may be helpful to apply some creativity here. For instance, not all your mentors have to be near or even alive. I have yet to meet in person some of the men and women who have greatly influenced my life. For the time being, they are part of the "cloud of witnesses" cheering me on in my own race of faith. The point is that it's not necessary to limit yourself to simply those who are alive and near.)

17

Reflections on 3:1–3

IDENTITY SHAPED BY THE SPIRIT

MANY IN our generation suffer from an identity crisis. The very advice, "Find your true self," signals that there's no shortage of people who are unable to answer confidently who they are, what they believe in, and how they ought to live. Given this struggle, which is not at all unique to our generation, today's passage is a much needed reminder of who we are in Christ Jesus. Thus, as Saint Paul notes, "to write the same things to you is not a burden for me but a safeguard for you" (3:1).

Before tackling what appears to be a belligerent verse (3:2), it's helpful to begin with the positive assertions in 3:3: "For we are the circumcision, who worship by the Spirit of God and boast in Christ Jesus and place no confidence in the flesh." In the Old Testament, circumcision was given to Father Abraham as a marker for the true people of God. What's extraordinary here is that Paul would assert that *we*—that is, the Gentiles who were generally considered in the Old Testament as those outside of God's people—are the circumcision in contrast to those who promote Jewish rituals. The basic reminder in 3:3, a reminder that every generation needs, is that it is those who boast in Christ—who place no confidence in their good (or bad) deeds but rather who glory in what Christ has accomplished through his life and death—belong to the people of God. In a sense, according to Paul, Christian (Gentile) believers have become the new true Jews. In passing we should observe how extraordinary it was for Paul, who was thoroughly trained in Jewish law, to make this statement. How profoundly the gospel must have reshaped his view of the world!

In the reflections to follow, we'll explore more deeply the contrast of boasting in Christ versus in the flesh. Here, we'll focus on the phrase "who worship by the Spirit of God." Paul's point here is that worship is not an external matter, but an internal one; worship that is pleasing and acceptable to God must be done in the Spirit, which is possible only for those who have become united to Christ by faith. The mention of the "Spirit of God" is really a reference to the new age of salvation wherein the Holy Spirit is poured out on God's people. The phrase at hand is, then, is a positive way of identifying those who are now part of this new age through their relationship with Jesus Christ. In other words, believers are people with a new citizenship, who belong to a new era characterized by hope, life, and the Spirit. Who am I? I am a citizen of heaven who through faith in Christ belongs to a new order. There should be no confusion and doubt about this rich and fundamental identity.

Given these convictions, Paul places the triple beware signs: "Beware of those dogs, beware of those evildoers, beware of those mutilators" (3:2). Paul's diction here is certainly somewhat inflammatory. No one likes to be called a dog, evildoer, or mutilator. But the terms here carry different connotations from what most have in mind. "Dog" was an Old Testament term to describe Gentiles. "Evildoer" isn't another term for Dr. Evil, but for those who promote good works (specifically what is taught in the Mosaic Law) with the belief that such works provide grounds for boasting before God. Similarly, "mutilators" refers to those that suppose any Jewish ritual (here, circumcision) contributes in some sense to salvation. In summary, Paul's concern is that the believers in Philippi would begin to get their cues concerning identity from those who were not believers, who held to beliefs diametrically opposed to the gospel, and who did not belong to the new order of the Spirit. Watch out for such people much in the way you would watch out for falling rocks, speeding vehicles, and financial scams.

Paul began this section by stating, "To write the same things to you is not a burden for me but a safeguard for you." There is perhaps no reminder more apt for believers today who listen carefully to the world concerning what is precious, good, and worthwhile to purse. Of course a six-digit salary necessitates a six-digit lifestyle! Of course sex outside of marriage is perfectly normally—who wants to be the forty-year-old virgin! Of course life is all about upgrading and advancing—lest you become the nice guy who finishes last! Given the widespread and profound influence of the world, we must beware of finding our identity, worth, and values from those who are not believers rather than from the gospel of Christ Jesus.

Questions for Further Reflection

1. Consider how you view yourself. What is the basis for your identity and values? Do your self-worth and values come from the gospel or the world? Like Saint Paul, has your view of the world, including yourself, been radically reshaped by the gospel?

2. Meditate on 3:3. How does it help you answer the question of identity? How would knowing this identity change the way you're dealing with immediate struggles? For instance, how does knowing that you belong to the people of God, that you're a citizen of heaven, that your boasting is in the work of Christ alone influence your struggle with singleness or unemployment?

3. Identify the "dogs, evildoers, and mutilators" in your life? How do they continue to shape the way you view yourself and make priorities? What would "watching out" for these people and things look like concretely in your life?

18

Reflections on 3:4–8

A CONVERSION OF VALUE

PHILIPPIANS 3:7–11 is one of the most extraordinary passages of Scripture, providing us much insight both into the essence of the gospel and Saint Paul's personal transformation. Scholars sometimes minimize Paul's own conversion experience, highlighting the dimension of the apostle's calling to the Gentiles. But there's perhaps no passage in Paul's letters that indicates more clearly that a total conversion—a radical transformation in worldview—took place upon encountering Jesus on the Damascus road. Today we'll focus on 3:4–8; the next two reflections on 3:9–11. Admittedly, this is somewhat of an unnatural break given verses 8–11 form a single sentence in Greek. The weight of glory, however, expressed in 3:9–11 is so great that it merits, at the very least, further reflections.

A clear progression takes place in 3:7–8. First, the shift in the verb "consider" from the perfect to the present tense ("I have considered a loss," 3:7; "I consider" a loss, 3:8) is intended to communicate Paul's personal sentiment, "In the past I considered all things a loss compared to the surpassing greatness of knowing Christ Jesus, and even now—despite all the troubles surrounding me—I still consider all things a loss." In short, the years of pain and suffering have not shaken his initial decision to give himself entirely to Christ. Second, there's a movement from the things that Paul formerly considered gain (3:4–6) to "all things" (3:8) to make the point that absolutely nothing compares to knowing Christ. Similarly, there's a development from the phrase "I consider loss" to "I have suffered a loss" to "I reckon them dung" to make the point that not only are the former things less attractive to him, they are now repugnant to him, for they stood in the way of recognizing his complete dependence on God's grace for salvation. Given this clear progression in thought and the use of such forceful language, we can hardly downplay the fact that Paul had experienced a true conversion. Imagine considering as dung all those things you formerly held to be most important! Wouldn't you agree that nothing less than a conversion is in view?

We shouldn't conclude that Paul suddenly disregarded his Jewish background and achievements as inherently worthless and objectionable. To set the stage for the gospel message in 3:7–11, Paul (reluctantly) recites his resume in 3:4–6. Without going into the details of each item, it'll suffice to note that Paul appreciated the value of his unique Jewish heritage and his incredible individual achievements. In short, Paul recognized that he was "cream of the crop," a recognition that he never became oblivious to, even while confessing the surpassing worth of Christ Jesus. However, as they resulted in pride and thus stood in the way of recognizing his need for a Savior, he considered them liabilities as worthless and repugnant as dung.

There's a way to read this passage incorrectly. If we take it to mean that Paul gave up a better life for a noble cause, we miss the point because glory is given to Paul versus the object of his new affections. Paul's threefold repetition of Christ—". . . I have considered a loss on account of Christ . . . I consider a loss for the surpassing greatness of knowing Christ Jesus . . . I reckon dung that I may gain Christ"— is intended to highlight the infinite worth of Christ; that Christ is so great that no loss is really in view relative to what has been gained. It's like someone "surrendering" his old car for a brand new Ferrari or a person giving up the cans she's collected for bars of gold. Paul's point here is that he has gladly forfeited literally all things to gain the pearl of greatest price. Like any rational investor, he has chosen what is of greatest value, what has brought him incomparable joy and, consequently, an unending supply of power to persevere in the face of all trial and tribulation.

Questions for Further Reflection

1. Do you tend to think of the Christian life in terms of what you have gained or have lost? Do you find yourself dwelling on the better life that could have been had you not committed your life to Christ (e.g., I could have had more friends, more possessions, more freedom to do whatever, whenever) or on the new hope and joy that is now yours?

2. List some of the things that were very important to you prior to becoming a Christian (e.g., popularity, financial success/security, marriage). How have they changed in value upon your becoming a Christian? If they haven't

changed substantially, what might this suggest about the authenticity of your conversion?

3. Reflect on how you have been trained with respect to the Christian faith. Has your conversion and growth come about mainly through fear ("Do you want to suffer eternally in hell?"), manipulation ("You can have your best life now if you let Jesus Christ into your heart"), or truth ("Christ Jesus is the pearl of greatest price such that everything is worthless compared to knowing him")?

19

Reflections on 3:9

JUSTIFIED BY FAITH

VERSES 9–11 pick up the train of thought from the closing statement of 3:8 ("that I may gain Christ"); that is, Saint Paul details what has been gained. As we've noted already, salvation has several aspects: justification (righteousness through faith, 3:9); sanctification (personal transformation through participation in the power of the resurrection and suffering, 3:10); and glorification (resurrection of the body, 3:11). All these blessings come as a result of being "found in him" (3:9a); this is the central motif in Paul's theology, hence his willingness—his gladness—to forfeit all things for the sake of gaining Christ. Today, however, we'll focus on the aspect of justification, a precious truth regularly forgotten by the church.

Verse 9 appears to adopt a poetic structure following an A-B-A' pattern (often described in the academic world as a *chiasm*). The A and A' bookends are antitheses, contrasting the righteousness that a person possesses through his/her effort to observe the law and the righteousness that comes from God and depends on faith. The repetition of the important preposition "from" ("from the law," 3:9a, "from God," 3:9c) is intended to accentuate this contrast. In putting forth this distinction, Paul is expressing that he has given up altogether on establishing a righteousness based on his own efforts—on the flesh (3:4–6)—and now looks externally to God, the righteous One who bestows righteousness to all who trust fully in Jesus Christ.

At the center of the pattern, which initiates the thought in the A′ element, Paul highlights that saving righteousness comes to the one who has faith in Christ Jesus. There has been a myriad of scholastic activity that argues for a translation something along the lines of, "the righteousness through the faithfulness of Christ." No one will deny that Christ's perfect obedience—his faithfulness to God's will even to the point of death—was necessary for our salvation. However, it should be noted that Paul nowhere speaks of Jesus in terms of being faithful but rather speaks of people placing their faith in Jesus Christ. Moreover, the context makes clear that Paul has in view the idea of believing wholly in Christ, placing one's complete confidence in him and only in him.

I've chosen to dwell on this particular aspect of salvation because over the years I've become increasingly convinced that many believers hold a "Santa Claus theology." We suppose that God relates to us on the basis of our performance. If things are going badly, we conclude that God is punishing us for the wrong we've done. If things are going well, we conclude that God is rewarding us for our righteous deeds. The problem with all this is that the beautiful truth of justification—that righteousness is an external gift from God received by faith versus that which comes by observing the law—is thrown out the window.

In other words, although many of us would profess to believe that righteousness is from God and depends on faith, functionally we still relate to God as if personal salvation comes from observing God's law. I'm not at all advocating a licentious lifestyle since salvation comes from grace instead of works. My point is that our relationship with God would be revolutionized—it would be filled with and driven by joy—if we fully embraced Paul's teaching on justification. God's righteousness does not come to those who deserve it, who have earned it by their own effort, but to those who admit their spiritual bankruptcy, surrender the things they formerly built their lives on (3:4–6), and trust fully in the One who alone lived a perfectly righteous life for our sake.

Questions for Further Reflection

1. Describe some subtle ways you live as if God's acceptance depends on your performance and good works versus faith in Jesus Christ.

2. What are some possible struggles you face in accepting the gospel truth that salvation comes not to those who try to be good but to those who trust entirely in Jesus Christ? Consider how this approach to salvation takes away from the glory of Christ.

3. In light of our discussion on the blessing of justification that comes through becoming one in Jesus, explain why Saint Paul would consider all things a loss compared to knowing Christ? Explain how the gospel breaks the grips of the things of this world—not through guilt—but through the beauty of Christ.

20

Reflections on 3:10

KNOWING CHRIST IN POWER AND SUFFERING

Saint Paul has forsaken all things formerly valuable (3:7–8) not only to gain a righteousness that comes through faith in Jesus Christ but also, as today's passage indicates, "to know him, that is, to know the power of his resurrection and the fellowship of his sufferings, becoming like him in his death" (3:10). This is a dense verse, one that is especially hard to understand given the extent to which the health-and-wealth gospel has quietly made its way into our thinking and outlook, so much so that suffering for the gospel is perceived by believers as an anomaly. We do our souls much good by reflecting deeply on the meaning of knowing Christ, as it's defined here in terms of sharing both in the power of the resurrection and the fellowship of Christ's sufferings.

Believers today tend to have "trivia knowledge" of Christ Jesus that boils down to praying John 3:16. In stark contrast, Paul understands "knowing him" in terms of a personal and powerful identification with Christ's death and resurrection, i.e., sanctification, which is nothing less than a complete personal transformation. Yesterday's reflection on justification might have left the impression that Paul advocates a licentious approach to life—as if we're now free to live however we please. The reference here, however, to "the *power* of his resurrection and the *fellowship* of his sufferings" means a commitment to pursue a new life marked by resurrection power (power to do God's will) and fellowship with the Savior. In short, knowing Christ is a complete identification with him not at all dissimilar to the commitment a husband and wife make to each other when exchanging their wedding vows. Such a commitment is essentially a declaration that neither one of the two will continue to live as singles, but as two committed people who will share in every season of joy and suffering.

Admittedly, Paul sounds somewhat masochistic when he says that he has surrendered all things to know the sufferings of Christ and to "become like him in his death." This take on Paul, however, may reflect our own naïve understanding of intimate relationships. Whether we're speaking of marriage or friendship, any such commitment involves the surrender of some joy and comfort to share in suffering and pain. That some of us disassociate suffering from discipleship may help us perceive how the health-and-wealth has permeated our own thinking.

The meaning of "becoming like him in his death" is twofold. On the one hand, there's the sense in which God's chosen people have died to sin once and for all through Christ's own death: by baptism his death is now our death. On the other hand, there's also the sense in which we continue to die as we mature through sanctification. Whenever we refuse to give in to the temptations we face regularly, whether it is lust, bitterness, or materialism, we're becoming more like him by dying to the old self and walking in newness of life. Similarly, we become increasingly like him in our sufferings for the gospel. Those who claim to know Christ but persist in living as they please and aspire to a life devoid of pain and suffering must remember that Christian salvation entails not only justification but also sanctification—the pursuit of a new life characterized by a complete identification with the One who suffered but ultimately conquered sin and death.

Questions for Further Reflection

1. Saint's Paul's understanding of salvation is rich with meaning, including not only the notion of "getting saved" (justification) but also of being transformed into the image of Christ (sanctification). How does your view of salvation measure against Paul's rich understanding? How does the apostle challenge you to expand your understanding of salvation?

2. Faith in Christ is not merely a way to get out of hell but a commitment analogous to the commitment established and enjoyed in marriage. How does your lifestyle reflect this understanding of the Christian life?

3. What does "becoming like him in his death" look like for you? What are some sins you have been battling as an expression of your commitment to Christ? In what ways are you suffering for the sake of the gospel?

21

Reflections on 3:11

GLORIFICATION: HOPE AND HUMILITY

IN YESTERDAY'S reflection we noted how Saint Paul's identification with Jesus includes "the fellowship of his sufferings, becoming like him in his death" (3:10). Taken in isolation, this might suggest that Paul had an unhealthy obsession with martyrdom or was perhaps even a masochist. We must remember, however, that Paul suffered as one with hope, i.e., Paul didn't suffer thinking that *perhaps* good will ultimately come out of it. Rather, as noted in Romans 8:17, "We suffer with him *in order* that we may also be gloried with him." In our suffering, then, as followers of Jesus Christ there is the sure hope of sharing in his glory, dubbed in 3:11 as "the resurrection from the dead." This represents the third aspect of Paul's understanding of salvation—the wonderful truth of glorification.

We know from Romans 8:18–30 that Paul doesn't have in mind just his own bodily resurrection. At the time of his personal resurrection, all creation will be renewed. There will be no more sorrow, no more pain, no more death, and no more disease. This will be the day when Paul, and all who have trusted fully in Jesus and have therefore persevered in the faith, will be vindicated and experience joy unimaginable. Christian suffering for the gospel never takes place in a vacuum, but in the abundant hope of resurrection glory. For this reason, as believers we weep in this life, we suffer, and ultimately die—but as people who weep, suffer, and die with hope that no one and nothing can take away!

Verse 11 exhibits an apprehension that we don't want to minimize. Instead of writing "*in order* to attain the resurrection from the death," Paul writes, "*if somehow* . . ." On the one hand, we mustn't think that Paul lacked assurance of his future glory. In many other Pauline passages, he makes clear that believers enjoy the sure hope of redemption. On the other hand, we don't want to minimize the obvious tentativeness evident in Paul's language. It may be that Paul is guarding the Philippians from misinterpreting the previous verses (3:8–10) as if he were suggesting that one could attain perfection in this life (see the subsequent verses). It may also be that Paul is reiterating the juxtaposition of divine sovereignty and human responsibility (see 2:12). Indeed, God cannot lie; therefore, those who trust in him will also experience the resurrected glory of Christ Jesus (2:9). Christian hope, in this sense, is sure. Still, we mustn't ever become presumptuous by supposing that because the object of our hope is unfailing, we are to be careless in the way we live. Rather, following in the steps of the apostle, we're to watch over our souls and continue to work out our salvation with fear and trembling that we may, somehow, attain the resurrection from the dead.

Paul's confident expectation of glory coupled with caution is a much needed challenge for us today. We know of many believers (perhaps we ourselves are guilty of this) who are too assured of their salvation, perhaps from a retreat experience or from having come from a Christian household, but who fail to watch over the state of their souls. Paul's point here is that while we should not second-guess the object and giver of our hope, we should not be overly confident about our own spiritual self-assessment. Rather, we do well to adopt a cautious attitude, which expresses itself in a vigilant watch over our souls and a diligent pursuit of holiness. This, at least, appears to be the tenor adopted by the apostle.

Questions for Further Reflection

1. Saint Paul's understanding of salvation is rich with meaning, including not only the notion of "getting saved" (justification) and being transformed into the image of Christ (sanctification), but also of participating in Christ's glorification. How does your view of salvation measure against Paul's rich understanding? How does the apostle challenge you to expand your understanding of salvation?

2. What distinguishes the way Christians suffer from the way all other people suffer? What does it mean for a believer to weep like those who have hope?

3. Being supremely confident in the One who has promised us eternal life is different from being unduly confident that we will share in glory. Do you live with this sort of sobriety? In what ways are you actively working out your faith to make sure your own salvation?

22

Reflections on 3:12–16

GRACE-STRIVINGS TOWARD THE GOAL

"NOBODY'S PERFECT." So we say. But isn't it the case that oftentimes we live as though we are perfect. This is most evident in the way we respond to criticism. Our defensiveness reveals how many of us do, in fact, believe that we are perfect. Why else would we be so stunned and offended by criticism?

In the first half of today's passage, Saint Paul reiterates by way of parallel A-B-A'-B' statements that he has hardly reached perfection. (Perhaps he found this necessary to say given his strong comments in the 3:9–11 may have left the impression that he thought he had attained perfection.) Verses 12a and 13a make up the negative affirmations (A, A'), highlighting that Paul has yet to reach resurrection glory—the redemption of our physical bodies and the perfection of our souls: "Not that I have already obtained this or am already perfect" (3:12a); "Brothers, I myself do not reckon that I have overtaken it." These negative statements are coupled with positive affirmations (B, B'), highlighting Paul's determination to press on: "I press forward to overtake it, even as I have been overtaken by Christ" (3:12b); "I pursue on toward the goal of the upward call of God in Christ Jesus" (3:13b–14). The imagery Paul uses is that of a runner (or, more generally, an athlete) pressing forward to win the prize by forgetting what is behind. Here again (see 3:11) we hear a note of tentativeness in Paul's language, reminding us that Paul never falls into a mode of complete self-reliance.

What hope, however, do believers have that they will attain the prize? Are they to rely on their efforts alone? Verse 14 balances Paul's caution with confidence because of the Lord Jesus Christ. The term "upward call" is an expression of God's divine calling upon his life, which—as noted earlier in the letter (1:6)—guarantees that God will bring to completion every good work he has started. In addition, the concluding prepositional phrase "in Christ Jesus" expresses that all the apostle's efforts are "grace-strivings," that is, efforts that are possible as a result of his union with his Lord and Savior. Our confidence, then, in running with perseverance is that God will ultimately enable and ensure us of final victory.

Such humility and hope should characterize all believers, especially those who suppose that they have already been perfected (3:15a). Even if others do not share fully in Paul's humble disposition, the apostle is confident that in due time God will reveal the truth of what he is saying (3:15b). Meanwhile, all believers are to make every effort to live according to the truth that they have already received (3:16). In particular, they are to adopt the humble mindset of Christ Jesus, which is theirs by virtue of their union with him. In passing, we should note how the apostle himself is practicing humility by allowing those who disagree with him time to grow. It's a good reminder for those who are truly mature to bear with those who think they are mature so that in time, according to God's will, they would truly attain maturity by walking in humility.

Questions for Further Reflection

1. How do you respond to criticism? How might your response be different if you adopted the apostle's perspective ("Not that I am already perfect")?

2. An important part of pressing on involves "forgetting what is behind," i.e., letting go of things in the past that might slow you down towards growing in holiness (notice that such things are not necessarily bad). What might God be challenging you to forget?

3. How does resting in God's faithfulness—that He will complete every good work he has started—bring encouragement as you run the race of faith?

23

Reflections on 3:17—4:1

WHOM DO YOU FOLLOW?

THE INSTRUCTIONS provided thus far in the letter, but especially in 3:12–16, concern how the Philippians, whom Saint Paul refers to as his beloved brothers—his desire, joy, and crown—are to stand firm in the Lord (4:1). In today's passage, Paul provides one additional encouragement to help them persevere in the face of persecution and difficulty. This encouragement focuses on the discipline of imitation: "Brothers, become imitators of me and pay attention to those who walk according to the example you have in us" (3:17). In other words, Paul is exhorting all believers to pay attention to who they pay attention to: to know who their role models are and to consider the outcome of their lives.

This encouragement is not given in a vacuum. Rather, it is with the apostle's awareness that "there are many who walk as enemies of the cross of Christ" (3:18). A description of whom Paul has in mind follows in verse 19, but the precise identity of the groups remains somewhat a mystery to biblical scholars. Some argue that Paul is referring to licentious people, others to Judaizers (given the thrust of the entire chapter). What can be said with a high degree of confidence is that this group has "minds set on earthly things" (3:19), which stands in stark contrast to those with a heavenly and Christlike mindset expressed in perseverance and service. As such, members of this group exhibit much pride and selfishness, qualities in clear opposition to the message of the cross.

Believers, however, are those not with minds buried in earthly matters but "who, as citizens of heaven, await a Savior, the Lord Jesus Christ" (3:20). As such, they ought not to follow those "whose end is destruction, whose god is their belly, and whose glory is in their shame," but those who live according to the hope that "our lowly bodies will be transformed to his body of glory according to the might that empowers him to subject all things to himself" (3:21). The latter elongated phrase of 3:21 highlights the greatness of Christ's power, which, in turn, ensures that those who eagerly await his return will not be ashamed; rather, God will complete the good work that has begun through the life, death, and resurrection of Jesus Christ.

With such great assurance and with the example of godly men and women, all believers are to "thus stand firm in the Lord." This passage is another reminder of how important it is for us to live intentionally as citizens of heaven. Specifically, Paul calls our attention to those whom we aspire to follow. Some naïvely suppose that they're truly independent people without realizing that there isn't a road that hasn't already been walked. Most passively accept the idols of our culture. Paul's challenge to us today, as people who live in hope of future glory, is to make a conscious decision to identify those who live as models of Christ and to walk in their ways.

Questions for Further Reflection

1. Who are your "real" role models? Take a moment to set aside the "right" answers (e.g., my Sunday school teacher) and consider how you spend your time and money. Do such decisions reflect the values of those who walk as diligent followers of Christ?

2. Describe the "enemies of the cross of Christ" in your life. That is, consider those who are so earth-minded that they cause you to forget your heavenly citizenship. In what ways have they influenced your life? What concrete steps are you taking to check their influence?

3. Describe those who follow in the example of Paul and Christ. How has their hope of glory been expressed concretely in their lives? How has their example inspired you?

24

Reflections on 4:2-3

THE MINDSET OF CHRIST IN CONFLICT

THIS PASSAGE, which begins with a personal exhortation to specific members among the Philippians—"I exhort Euodia and I exhort Syntyche to have the mindset of Christ" (4:2)—might strike us as somewhat unusual, given Saint Paul didn't regularly "call out" specific persons by name in his letters. We can perhaps better appreciate the force of the exhortation if we remember that Paul's letters were read aloud before entire congregations. One can only imagine what it must have felt like to have the apostle single certain persons out in the form of a rebuke. But the fact that Paul is able to do so tells us something about both his closeness and comfort with the Philippians and the maturity of these women and the Philippian community as a whole. Despite his public rebuke, Paul holds these women in high esteem as reflected in the description, "these women have contended beside me for the sake of the gospel" (4:3). While Paul doesn't go so far as to recognize them as pastors or elders, the use of the term "fellow workers" indicates that these women played a significant—likely public—role in the church.

Paul's exhortation to these women echoes the theme that he has been sounding throughout this letter: to adopt the humble mindset of Jesus Christ (2:5). Some popular translations read "to agree in the Lord," leaving the impression that Paul is exhorting them to get along or perhaps to come to an agreement. Given Paul's pastoral experience with many churches, surely he wasn't so naïve to suppose that leaders can come to a simple agreement. What the apostle seems concerned with is not with the actual disagreement but with the underlying attitude. In 2:1–4, he exhorts the entire community to consider others more significant than themselves and to look primarily to the interests of others. It appears that these great women of faith forgot their fundamental calling to adopt a meek and serving disposition towards each other during their difference, a mistake not uncommon even among the most mature of us. The following saying is a much needed reminder that we can disagree without becoming disagreeable, that we can differ without disposing of the mindset of Christ. Of course, it's always sobering to remember that differences between believers are temporary given their names are "in the book of life," i.e., given that someday they will live in perfect fellowship with God and one another. I imagine the nature of our conflicts would drastically change if we kept in mind this eternal perspective.

Paul's exhortation here, however, is not only for Euodia and Syntyche but also for the entire community in Philippi. Notice how Paul writes, "Genuine yokefellow, help these women." The context makes clear that he is urging the Philippians to help these women achieve reconciliation. In other words, the other believers in the community are not to take a passive stance, as if the discord at hand is merely between two individuals. Rather, they are to exhort these women—these leaders—to live out the gospel. This is a reminder to us that even godly people need the gospel and that believers are one body, such that any dysfunction between two members is a concern for the entire body.

Questions for Further Reflection

1. What lessons can be drawn from this seemingly simple exhortation/rebuke to Euodia and Syntyche, whether from the perspective of Paul or the Philippians?

2. All of us—church leaders and members alike—tend to forget their calling to adopt the humble mindset of Christ during conflicts. The way one missionary put it, "Those who are sinned against respond by sinning." How have you handled conflicts in the past? Do you forget that you are a believer, called to consider the preferences and interests of others above your own?

3. Reconciliation is a community affair. How does this challenge you to play a more active role in establishing peace within your church? How does this biblical truth challenge the tendency to "mind your own business"?

25

Reflections on 4:4–7

REJOICE: THE LORD IS NEAR

TODAY'S PASSAGE consists of several related commands, with the first having some prominence given its repetition in the letter. In verse 4, Saint Paul writes: "Rejoice in the Lord always. Again, I will say rejoice." The repetition—not only here but throughout the letter—of the command to "rejoice" clearly indicates that joy was becoming increasingly difficult to come by among the Philippians. This shouldn't surprise us given how they were undergoing external persecution and internal division. It's admittedly difficult to rejoice when all is not well. Nevertheless, the prepositional phrase "in the Lord" and adverb "always" remind us that joy can be an ever present reality for those who have united themselves to Christ through faith. The apostle himself has exemplified this reality throughout the letter. In passing we should note that joy isn't the product of passivity; rather, we must fight for joy—we must pursue it as we would pursue any good thing by fixing our eyes on the Lord, whose life and work make it possible to rejoice always.

Coupled with joy is a forbearing and gentle spirit; hence, the second exhortation, "Let your gentleness be known to all; the Lord is near" (4:5). Paul is reminding the Philippians that their presence should not be characterized by a downtrodden spirit and self-absorption. Rather, there should be a note of hope and thoughtfulness that is evident to all as a result of knowing that "the Lord is near." This statement can be a reference either to Christ's second coming or his constant presence in the life of believers through the Spirit (or both). The point is that his abiding presence and promise to return in glory empowers all believers to rejoice and continue in their service to all the saints and those in need.

Finally, Paul provides an immensely practical solution to the problem of anxiety, the great enemy of joy and thoughtfulness. Instead of being anxious about anything, the believers in Philippi are encouraged to adopt a robust prayer life, expressed in the multiple terms "prayer, petition, thanksgiving, requests." The apostle's intention here is not to present various nuances of prayer but to highlight the point that we ought to pray about anything and everything, now and always. Instead of pretending that all is well or keeping everything pent up, Paul encourages us to "let your requests be known to God" (4:6)—to talk to him because he cares for us much more than we'll ever know. And the promise we have is that "the peace of God that transcends all understanding will guard [our] hearts and minds in Christ Jesus" (4:7). Prayer, of course, is only impractical to the one who doesn't engage in the kind of prayer life described above. The apostle, however, is speaking from personal experience; and mature believers will say the same. God hears and comforts those who trust him by giving them a peace that only those who have pursued God in prayer understand. Such peace guards our hearts and minds from the suffocating power of anxiety and empowers us with overwhelming joy to serve those around us.

I especially appreciate this passage because of the way it relates joy, self-absorption, anxiety, and prayer. Life, of course, can't be simplified to a few formulas. But there's something to be said, that a life without prayer is often accompanied by anxiety, which, in turn, sucks the joy out of our existence and inclines us to wallow in our own fears and self-pity. On the other hand, those who have been united to Christ by faith and who know, therefore, that they can approach the throne of grace with confidence to make their requests known to God are empowered by the peace that transcends all understanding which, in turn, empowers them to serve all with complete humility and perseverance. May this peace overwhelm you today as you turn to him in prayer!

Questions for Further Reflection

1. In some sense joy is the product of obedience and persistence (notice how Paul commands them twice to rejoice). How does this challenge you in your own pursuit of joy?

2. How is anxiety the enemy of joy and selflessness? Reflect on some seasons in your life when this was especially the case.

3. Do you pray about anything and everything, now and always? Have you experienced the peace that is promised here to those who trust in the Lord? What concrete steps can you take to develop a more robust prayer life?

26

Reflections on 4:8–9

HEALTHY THINKING

Prior to his final teaching on giving, Saint Paul provides one additional encouragement to the Philippians, a somewhat general encouragement but no less important than anything else he's written thus far. His encouragement here focuses on the coupling of the believer's thought life and practice.

Paul begins by reminding the Philippians to pay attention to what they pay attention to, i.e., to be self-aware of what kind of thoughts occupy their mind on a regular basis. To be sure, everyone in a sense is free to think whatever he/she pleases, but that's very different from supposing that all thoughts are equally healthy for the soul. For this reason, Paul exhorts the believers in Philippi to "think about whatever is honorable, whatever is just, whatever is pure, whatever is lovely, whatever is commendable—and whatever else is excellent and praiseworthy" (4:8). While this seems obvious, many of us can easily confess how our thoughts so easily get lost in regret, depression, anxiety, greed, and so forth. Given the apostle's prior comments on living like citizens of heaven, the encouragement here can be summarized as a call to think thoughts that are fitting for those who have been united to Christ by faith and now participate in a new order characterized by life in the Spirit.

There's a clear progression in 4:9. Lest the Philippians think of these virtues in an abstract way, Paul reminds them of how he and his colleagues exemplified in every sense the things that are excellent and praiseworthy; hence he writes, "What you have learned and received and heard and seen in me." In addition, Paul highlights that it's not enough to simply think about the good—as if he were saying, "Do as I say, not as I do." At the end of this statement Paul adds, "Practice these things," to make clear that thought and life should be inseparably tethered to each other, to the extent that believers should be able to say, "If you want to know what occupies my mind and consumes my heart—just look at my life." To those who find themselves saying, "I know what's right and good," Paul says, "Don't just claim to know the good—practice it!"

The closing statement of verse 9, "And the God of peace will be with you," echoes 4:7 with an important nuance. Paul reminds the Philippians that it isn't just the peace of God that is given to those who seek him in prayer. Rather, God gives himself through the Holy Spirit. This is an inspiring reminder of the intensely personal nature of the Christian faith. We're not simply following a set of principles and beliefs; on a more basic level, we are following a person who has promised never to leave or abandon us, whether we're wrongly imprisoned like Paul or facing persecution and trouble. To be sure, when we fail to guard our minds, the anxieties of life begin to overwhelm us, leading us to think that God has abandoned us. Paul reminds us here, however, that the God of peace remains with his people as they strive to grow into the image of Christ. Through such a promise we find power to persevere with joy in all our service.

Questions for Further Reflection

1. Reflect on your thought life. Do you tend to guard your mind? Do you pay attention to what you pay attention to—to where your mind wanders? How does the apostle's exhortation to be intentional about what you think about challenge you? How does your current thought life contrast with verse 8?

2. Notice the emphasis Paul places on action: "Practice these things!" Do you find yourself often saying, "I know, I know, I know," or are you regularly seeking to adjust your life according to the truths of the gospel you're learning and seeing in others?

3. Loneliness is a part of life that doesn't ever quite fully disappear, but that's different from actually being alone. How does the promise of God's abiding presence encourage you in your situation? What concrete difference should his promised presence have on the way you handle your struggles?

27

Reflections on 4:10–14

CONTENTMENT REGARDLESS
OF CIRCUMSTANCE

TODAY WE reflect in part on one of the most well known verses in the Bible, but perhaps also one of the most poorly understood. Many have taken 4:13 to suggest a sort of indomitable faith—that one can do all things, literally, through Christ, whether it's boxing Mike Tyson, passing an exam without studying, or winning a nation with the gospel. Now, there's something to be said of the kind of faith that believes in a God who is able to do far more than anything we ask or imagine (Ephesians 3:20, although even here there's no definitive suggestion that we can do the impossible). But at least in 4:13 Saint Paul does not have in mind herculean Christianity, but rather Christian contentment, a grossly underrated virtue.

The language of verses 11–12 might suggest that Paul was a Stoic: "Not that I am speaking because I am in need, for I have learned to be content in whatever situation. I know how to be brought low, I know how to abound. In all situations, I have learned the secret of being content. . . ." To be sure, Paul *is* saying that he has learned to transcend his current circumstances so that he's content whether well fed or hungry (which is no small feat!). But our passage also makes clear the circumstances—specifically, the actions of others believers—still made a difference for him. Notice in 4:10 and 4:14 how he expressed joy and gratitude for the concrete way in which the Philippians expressed their care for him, specifically for the gift they had sent through Epaphroditus. This is an important observation because sometimes we're tempted to think that "super-saints" don't need encouragement. We assume that they're doing well because they always seem well. We suppose that their relationship with God is so vibrant that our encouragement ultimately makes no difference on their overall health. Paul's joy on account of the Philippians' tangible expression of care reminds us that even "apostles" benefit greatly from our concrete acts of kindness that show we're thinking and praying for them.

Paul makes clear, however, that his commendation of the Philippians isn't some sort of passive-aggressive way to garner more support; rather, in 4:11, he highlights that he has learned to be content whatever the situation, which he explains further in 4:12. Paul was educated among the elite of his time. He was trilingual and his letters reflect his training in rhetoric, philosophy, and law. In addition, there were likely times when Paul was able to wine and dine with wealthy Christians. At the same time, Paul also knew what it felt like to go to sleep hungry, to be isolated and treated like a criminal, and to wonder whether he would have enough to make it through the next season. Many people know either abundance or poverty; Paul knew both. But the one thing he had discovered in these opposite situations was that Christ remained the same and brought satisfaction and strength independent of circumstance; hence, the declaration, "I can do all things through [Christ] who strengthens me." That is, I can be content in any and every situation because Christ is with me, giving me supernatural strength to persevere with joy. And this secret of being content is available to all who unite themselves to Christ by faith. It is this secret that enables us to rejoice always and to persevere in serving God by serving the saints.

Questions for Further Reflection

1. How many Christians do you personally know that display the quality of Christian contentment? Are you marked by contentment? Why do you think this is such a difficult virtue to come by?

2. Who is a "super-saint" that might benefit from your tangible expression of care? What concrete acts of kindness can you show him/her? Commit to doing so.

3. Have you learned the secret of being content in every situation? Describes examples from your life when you were able to persevere with joy through Christ. How do these examples encourage you as you look ahead to new trials?

28

Reflections on 4:15–20

CHRIST-PATTERNED GIVING

MONEY IS a constant concern for almost everyone, and closely related to money is the question of giving: how much should I give to the Lord? Do I tithe from my gross or net income? Does my giving change as my salary bracket changes? Saint Paul provides us some principles to keep in mind with respect to this important topic. (I don't assume an order of importance in stating these principles.)

First, our giving should flow from our understanding of Christ's self-sacrifice. In verse 18, Paul describes the Philippians' gift as a "fragrant offering, a sacrifice pleasing and acceptable to God." What's stunning here is that this is almost the exact language he uses in Ephesians 5:2 to describe Christ's sacrifice ("a fragrant offering and sacrifice to God"). Obviously Paul isn't suggesting that any sacrifice we make is comparable to Christ's great sacrifice. But his point is that Christ's sacrifice should provide a pattern for all Christian giving. Specifically, Christ's example teaches us that all our giving demands some discomfort and even pain on our part. The question really isn't whether I should tithe from my gross or net income. Rather, the question is whether I've given to the point of experiencing some level of discomfort. Only this sort of giving is consistent with the nature of Christ's self-sacrifice.

Second, our giving should flow from our experience of Christ's self-sacrifice. Paul highlights the generous disposition of the Philippians, "that no church partnered with me in terms of giving and receiving except you alone" (4:15); "that even in Thessalonica you sent for my need again and again" (4:16); "that I have received all things and more, that I am amply supplied" (4:18a). Paul's interest is not in "receiving more gifts" (4:17), but, in part, to acknowledge the extent of their generosity. For the Philippians, giving wasn't a matter of meeting the bare minimum. Rather, it was giving—even if it came at a tremendous cost to them—to provide abundantly for the apostle. In my opinion, there are few things that provide better evidence of one's experience of God's generosity towards us than our generosity towards others.

Third, our giving should be done with full conviction that God is just and will not forget our material sacrifices for the sake of the gospel. Verse 17 concludes in perhaps an unsettling manner: "I seek the fruit that accrues to your account." Most of us are wary about supposing that there are gradations (classes) in heaven. Socio-economic differences seem to be a thing of this world. While I'm not sure there will be socio-economic levels in heaven, the Bible does seem to suggest—at the very least—there will be some kind of difference depending on how we have lived on earth. Paul's statement here indicates that God will "repay" all who have lived generously and sacrificially for the sake of the gospel. Surely it's not so far fetched to suppose that the one who has given generously in faith will have a larger account than the one who has been stingy and given bare minimum. Our giving, then, should be done knowing that God will honor our generosity.

Fourth, our giving should be done with full conviction that God will meet all our needs in this life (4:19). Of course, this doesn't mean that God will provide everything we think we need (we do, after all, use the word "need" somewhat carelessly). Oftentimes, by giving only what we need he teaches us what we really need. The reason we can be so confident in God's provisions is that he has already given to us abundantly in Jesus Christ. If he did not withhold his Son, how can we doubt that he will not also graciously give us all things?

Finally, our giving should be done with the purpose of bringing glory to "our God and Father" (4:20). The ultimate purpose for every person is to glorify God and enjoy him forever. When we give in a way that shows that God—not financial security—is ours and that he is more precious than any material thing, we glorify him as the most glorious One.

Question for Further Reflection

1. Meditate on the principles of giving provided in this passage. How are you challenged to approach giving differently? List concrete ways God is calling you to change in this area of money and generosity.

29

Reflections on 4:21–23

GREETINGS TO AND FROM ALL BELIEVERS

I N A sense, there's not much to say on the closing of Paul's letter to the Philippians. It contains greetings and a final blessing, which we find in all his letters. So in this final reflection, we'll simply make some general comments regarding unity in Christ Jesus, echoing some of the themes we have seen in the letter.

Verse 21 begins with the command to "Greet every saint in Christ Jesus." We know already that the community in Philippi was experiencing conflict. This is implied in Paul's exhortation to the community to look not only to one's own interest, but also to the interest of others (2:1–4). This is made explicit in 4:2 where Saint Paul urges Euodia and Syntyche to approach their disagreement in a manner consistent with the humility and kindness of Christ. Also, we know that the community was experiencing some form of persecution. All this lends to a contentious environment where tempers flare and personalities clash. Usually in such a setting the first thing to go is a basic hello between believers. For this reason, the otherwise bland command to

"Greet every saint in Christ Jesus" is actually quite relevant and challenging.

The next two statements, "The brothers who are with me greet you," and, "All the saints greet you, especially those of Caesar's household," reminds the Philippians of their new family "in Christ Jesus." Paul points to both those brothers who are currently beside him and then, more generally, to all the saints to reiterate the point that personal salvation includes adoption into God's family, a family that goes beyond the borders of our immediate church community. Many churches are guilty of being unduly territorial while forgetting that we are all fellow "saints" (notice its occurrences in both 4:21 and 4:22), united to one another through Christ Jesus. We ought to rejoice when other churches "succeed" (using the term loosely) and pray for and help those churches that are struggling. The competition we see in the business world between companies in the same industry should be altogether absent within the Christian community.

The letter concludes with the blessing, "The grace of the Lord Jesus Christ be with your spirit." "Grace" is to be understood not only as a reference to God's unmerited kindness, but also to God's empowering presence. Those who have united themselves to Christ by faith can rest assured that God's abiding presence in the Holy Spirit will remain with them, giving them peace, contentment, and power to persevere with joy in their service for the gospel. May we continue to look to the One who will be faithful to complete the good work he has begun in us!

Questions for Further Reflection

1. How do you interact with believers in your immediate church community with whom you have a conflict? On the most basic level, do you greet them with the peace of Christ? How does the closing of Paul's letter to the Philippians challenge you to approach such individuals differently?

2. How does something as simple as a greeting to an "enemy" reflect our gospel convictions?

3. Does your church adopt a collegial spirit with other churches that confess Jesus as Lord and Savior? If so, how does your church express mutual support and respect?